MW01621172

Ancient Secrets of Success

The Four Truths Revealed

Tulshi Sen

Ancient Secrets of Success
The Four Truths Revealed
by Tulshi Sen

ISBN 978-0-9809602-7-3

Formerly Published as Ancient Secrets of Success for Today's World
First Printing in Canada, 2006

Published by Omnisun Systems Inc.
405-195 Lake Driveway W., Toronto, ON, Canada, L1S 7H7

For information please visit:

https://tulshisen.com

To
The Master Within

CONTENTS

PART ONE
Preparation for Success

PART TWO

The Applications Of The Ancient Secrets Of Success

I can't help but laugh when

I hear the fish in the water is thirsty.

\- Kabir Sahib

"Human knowledge and skills alone cannot lead humanity to a happy and dignified life"

...Albert Einstein

Our time is distinguished by wonderful achievements in the fields of scientific understanding and the technical application of those insights. Who would not be cheered by this?

But let us not forget that knowledge and skills alone cannot lead humanity to a happy and dignified life. Humanity has every reason to place the proclaimers of high moral standards and values above the discoverers of objective truth. What humanity owes to personalities like Buddha, Moses, and Jesus ranks for me higher than all the achievements of the enquiring and constructive mind.

What these blessed men have given us we must guard and try to keep alive with all our strength if humanity is not to lose its dignity, the security of its existence, and its joy in living.

\- Albert Einstein

PART ONE

PREPARATION FOR SUCCESS

CHAPTER 1

ORIGIN AND SOURCE OF THE SECRETS REVEALED

The Author's Note

Today we live in a world of multitasking and attention crisis. Most of the world is caught in the quick sand of a hurried anxiety-ridden life; with no apparent life line to grasp on to for safety. Whether you are a CEO of a gigantic multinational corporation or a CEO of a family, an office worker or a homemaker, all alike are equally lost in the info swamp of day to day living.

Ancient Secrets of Success is for those who at times feel trapped and see no way out; whether they are surrounded by prosperity and want more from life or are in search of prosperity to complete their life. It is for those who want to live a life of abundance, without hard work, and without the deafening tumult of anxiety that so often accompanies the search for prosperity. The Ancient Secrets bring both abundance and joy as they are both necessary for a full and a complete life.

The Ancient Secrets have their roots in the teachings of the Masters of Antiquity. These teachings go as far into the past as Hermes of Ancient Egypt, the *Vedas* of India, and the *Bible*. These teachings turned ordinary people into heroes, kings, and emperors. They became leaders, romantics, and visionaries who changed the world. These teachings are ageless, practical, and down to earth. They are for everyone and anyone who wants to take command of their life and mold it to their heart's desire.

There is a Chinese saying that a picture is worth a thousand words. This is true, but a story is worth a thousand pictures. The Spirit of man, the individualized Universal Spirit, does not speak or understand ordinary, everyday language. The language of the Soul or Consciousness is pictures, images, parables, metaphors, stories, and myths. That is why the Masters used these instruments to speak directly to the Spirit of man. That is also why *Ancient Secrets of Success* contains many metaphors, parables, and stories. They prepare you for practical application of the Secrets.

These stories and parables do not originate from the author nor does he claim them to be his. Most of these stories are folklore and Ancient tales of the world that have been passed down from the ages.

These teachings also do not belong to the author or originate from him; he has sat at the feet of the Master and under his guidance researched these Ancient Secrets from cultures and traditions across the world. He has extracted out the essence of the teachings and made it into a tincture for those who want to be successful.

There are two types of tinctures. The first type covers the surface and does not enter the depth of an object; it is like a thin veneer. The Masters have only repulsion for this type of tincture. The second type of tincture transforms the object into the tincture. This type of tincture soaks into the individual and he becomes the teachings. All theories, all speculations, and all hypotheses will fall off like rocket boosters falling off a space craft once it has freed itself from Earth's gravity. So too will the individual, with the understanding and practice of the Ancient Secrets, make a tincture for his success, immerse himself in it, and break away from the gravity of the ice cold intellect. He will then begin to live from his true Being.

To accomplish this objective easily and without much effort *Ancient Secrets of Success* has been divided in two parts. The first part befriends the mind and the intellect. It gives the intellect its rightful place. The intellect will realize that the foundation of its existence is Spirit, which is his Consciousness. Peace, Security, and Prosperity lie in total reliance on the Self. The Self is his Consciousness. The Mind can reach out and feel all it wants to feel. It can express life in all its grandeur and beauty. It can be in a place where there is no fear, no pain, no lack, and only unbounded abundance.

The mind is the totality of our memories and the intellect is the chooser and decision maker. Both are befriended by communicating with them in the language they understand, the language of stories, myths, and metaphors. This is the distilled essence of the wisdom of the teachings, not mere superficial theory.

The second part of *Ancient Secrets of Success* pours out the nectar of the Ancient Secrets for the mind and intellect to drink to their heart's content. The mind and intellect become disciples of Spirit, our Consciousness. This is accomplished through practical applications; through a system of meditation, as practiced by great emperors, kings, heroes, and poets of the past. This nectar of life tinges every fiber of the practitioner's Being. He realizes the meaning of an Ancient declaration from the *Upanishads*. It is no longer a piece of poetry for him, to immerse into euphoria with, but becomes his Being.

> *That is Infinite. This is Infinite. From that Infinite arises This Infinite. This Infinite is brought forth from That Infinite and That Infinite remains Infinite.*
>
> - Isha Upanishad

CHAPTER 2

TRUE SUCCESS AND MISTAKEN SUCCESS

What Is Success?

Having unlimited wealth does not make you successful, it makes you rich. Having fame does not make you successful, it makes you famous. Though one must be rich and famous if they want to be, and it is good, true success is when you have full control over your thinking process. This may sound mundane to you if you are only looking for riches and fame now. But take this to heart; you can be as rich and famous as you want to be if you know how to be successful.

The yardstick of success is not measured by fame and wealth; it is measured by your level of understanding of who you are, why you are here, and where are you going from here. Your measure of your success is your own happiness quotient.

They Have It All Upside Down

Those who seek wealth and fame because they do not have it now, will usually say, "Let me get wealth and fame first, and then I will dwell on the idea of controlling my mind and finding out the rest. My wealth and fame will give me the leisure of looking for myself."

They have it all upside down. If you know how to control your mind by realizing who you are, you can have all you want. You can be happy, wealthy, and famous. Then what you want to be will be up to you.

Many rich and famous people have given up their wealth and fame just to seek bliss and happiness. Many rich and famous people are in rehab centers and many have sold their happiness to lust and addictions and have become slaves to their mind. With all their fame and wealth they appear to be beggars, seeking scraps of happiness. Are they successful?

Trapped in a Midas Syndrome

The Ancient story of King Midas gives us a bird's eye view of such misery. The story goes that King Midas sought a boon, that whatever he touched would become gold. And he got that boon. He became rich, but this boon became intolerable to him. His daughter embraced him and she became gold. He touched his food and that become gold. He did not see the point of carrying on with this power. He went to more pains to get rid of this boon than he did to get the boon.

If you want to become wealthy then wealth must be a genuine desire in your heart. Seeking wealth for security's sake under the guise of becoming wealthy is not success. You will become like King Midas. You will see your children but you won't feel them. You will embrace your lover but you won't feel the euphoria that you want to feel in that embrace. You will dine in the most exclusive restaurants and be served the finest cuisine but you will not taste the food.

The Secrets of Success are in you now. Your Consciousness is a Touchstone and it can make gold at will. Unlike King Midas you have the ability to use the Touchstone when you choose to. Right now your stone is not under your control, it is under the possession of your mind. You have to reclaim it.

The Ancient Path to Success for Today's World

The Secrets of Success are in your heart. *Ancient Secrets of Success* is like a map. You need to study it and follow the path to find the secret. When you read, have some writing materials with you. You will not know when the secret will reveal itself. Make a note immediately as it arises; your mind will be reluctant to remember it for you.

Ancient Secrets of Success has two parts. The first part is the preparation for the search for the secrets and the second part is realizing the secrets and implementing them.

You will be given meditations and other exercises, follow them as well as you can. Do not concern yourself with whether you are doing it correctly or not. These are exercises you cannot do incorrectly. Your desire to be successful will lead you to the best way suitable for you.

Then you will be transported to a land of magic, color and vibrancy, and you will realize that the place that you lived all this time is not the same as you had perceived it to be.

The following story was told to me by my Master. It vividly paints a picture of how we typically live out our lives desiring to be successful and how we let our ego sabotage the opportunities that life presents to us to be a success. Our life is a Touchstone. We were born to experience the transcendent thrill of this Touchstone. It is totally different from the boon that King Midas sought and got.

CHAPTER 3

LIFE
IS
A TOUCHSTONE

The Story of How Success is Unwittingly Rejected

Once upon a time in a small village in a Himalayan valley lived a poor storekeeper. His store was the only store in this remote, isolated village far away from any town. The village was poor and so was the storekeeper.

A great Master was passing through the village and needed to stay there for three days. The poor storekeeper invited the Master to stay with him. The Master was pleased and the storekeeper, with the little he had, made the Master comfortable in his home as far as he could.

At the end of the three days when the Master was taking leave, the storekeeper fell at the feet of the Master and asked him for his blessings.

He said, "Master, please bless me that I can be rich. You yourself see now that the income from my store is not sufficient to support me and that my house is a hovel."

The Master blessed him and said, "I will do better than that. I will give you this stone and this stone is no ordinary stone. If you touch iron to this stone, the iron will instantly turn into gold. And by the way, I will leave this stone with you for the next three months. When I will be returning from my pilgrimage three months from now, I will take back this stone from you. You have three months to make yourself rich; as rich as you want to be."

The poor storekeeper was ecstatic and thanked the Master profusely. The Master continued on his journey.

The village was located in a very remote and a very isolated valley in the Himalayas. The nearest town was far away and the only way to get there was to trek through the mountains on foot. In that town a bazaar was held once a month and only once a month. In that bazaar there was only one iron merchant.

On the day of the bazaar of the first month the poor storekeeper made the long trek to the town, excited to become rich and live a very happy, luxurious life. The promise of the future hummed before him.

He straight away went to the iron store and asked the merchant the price of iron. The iron merchant told him the price of iron was going up and now it was nine Rupees for forty kilos. This enraged the poor storekeeper.

In his anger he said, “I am nobody’s fool. You are into profiteering; I will not let you have the satisfaction of fooling me. I will come back next month and then you will come to your senses and sell me the iron at the right price.” The storekeeper stomped out, still poor. Little did he realize how much just one kilo of gold would do to his poverty struck life.

Next month, the still poor storekeeper made his way to the bazaar. As he was approaching the iron merchant, he felt a sense of anger overwhelming him. The iron merchant saw him and said, “You should have bought your iron last month; the price has doubled and now it is eighteen Rupees for forty kilos.” The iron merchant gave him half a smile.

This infuriated the poor storekeeper even further and he felt that the iron merchant knew that he was desperate to buy the iron. He was not going to give the merchant the satisfaction of taking advantage of him. He also thought that if he held out for another month the merchant would buckle under and give him a fair price.

He said to the iron merchant, “I understand that you know how much I want to buy the iron, but you don’t know that I am not a fool. I can wait it out. I will come back next month and then you will have no choice but to sell me the iron at the right price.”

The day of the bazaar of the third month arrived and the still very poor storekeeper, with the anticipation of becoming rich, made his way to the marketplace. He asked the iron merchant, “You had a whole month to think. Are you ready to be fair and give me a fair price for your iron? I intend to buy all your iron.”

The merchant said, "I always offered you a fair price. I am sorry I have to disappoint you again. Now the price has gone up by another nine Rupees and now it is twenty seven Rupees for forty kilos." The merchant laughed and continued, "You should have bought it the first month you came."

This enraged the poor storekeeper. He totally lost his balance and walked out of the store saying, "Under no circumstances am I going to let you have the better of me." In his numbness of anguish, in his total immersion of living the mundane life, he became oblivious to the fact that he had now had the Touchstone for almost three months. And that this was his last month with the Touchstone and this was the last market day to get the iron.

In the meantime the Master finished his journey and remembered the poor storekeeper and his Touchstone. He also remembered that he had to pick up his Touchstone. As he entered the village he was looking for a well lit up store and all the signs of plenty and affluence. He could not find the store he was expecting to see, as he was still looking at the hovel.

The storekeeper saw the Master and came running to him with folded hands and greeted him.

The Master asked, "What happened? Why are you not rich already? Did you not find iron in the bazaar?"

The poor storekeeper replied, "Oh great Master, yes there was plenty of iron but the iron merchant kept raising the price on me. I could not let him have the better of me."

The Master said, “That is good but I must be on my way and I have come to collect my stone from you as your three months are over.”

The poor storekeeper gave him back the stone and the Master continued his return journey. The poor storekeeper remained poor.

Our Consciousness is our Touchstone. The three months are the three periods of our life, which are youth, middle age, and senior years. Then the Touchstone will be taken away by the Great Master. What we do with it during these three months is up to us.

CHAPTER 4

ANCIENT SECRETS OF SUCCESS

Success is commonly understood as setting and achieving goals. The Ancient Secrets proclaim that true success is the ability to set goals from the Absolute, from the Unconditioned, knowing that once the goal or vision is painted it is certain to manifest. The Beginning and Ending are one.

All our desires originate from a sense of lack or want of something or some condition. Then we have a tendency to figure out how we are going to fill the lack or want, given the conditions and our circumstances. That is, the fulfillment of our desire is dependent upon or is subject to the resources available to us.

If the desire does not fit the conditions or the resources, we reject the desire outright, and carry a sense of inadequacy with us. Or we alter the desire or water it down to fit the conditions and resources that are available to us. Then we go about fulfilling the altered want. This is setting a goal from the conditioned and not from the Absolute or the Unconditioned.

Stepping Out of the Box

A goal is a Vision. A conditioned goal is not creative. It is construction of a vision totally dependent on the resources available. We will see later that all creation is from the Absolute and the Unconditioned.

A Visionary sees not the conditions but sees what conditions he wants to have to fulfill his desire. Most of the world will consider him mad. The question is, who is really mad? Isn't it madness to live in a conditioned world while you know that your Consciousness is always in the Absolute and in the Unconditioned? Is not this the psychology of the prodigal son who left the center of his resources, his Father, to seek fortune in the Circumference or in the conditioned world? This is the power of the Universe resident in you. This thought will be elaborated in detail throughout *Ancient Secrets of Success.*

In Part Two of *Ancient Secrets of Success* you will be given the Four Proclamations and meditations which will enable you to combat your mind's dependency on conditions for setting goals and visions. The mind seems to be addicted to conditions and does not rely on the Absolute. The continuous onslaught of your mind's dependency on conditions is an addiction which suffocates your Consciousness.

Freeing Your Mind

Achieving the ability to set goals from the Absolute is the purpose of *Ancient Secrets of Success.* These secrets reveal how you can develop the capacity to set goals and visions from the heart, from the Unconditioned, from outside the box. Till we are able to achieve this state of mind all our goals are being set by us on the basis of our past experiences and present conditions. In the Ancient Vedic texts this is described as being trapped in Karma. Karma simply means action, and being trapped in Karma means that all our actions are a ripple effect of our previous actions. It is an endless chain of the same conditions and it appears there is no escape from its iron grip.

It is the ultimate desire of life to go where you have never gone before but unless we break free from this Karmic entrapment it is not achievable. To break free from this dependency on the past and build a brand new future is the purpose of the teachings of the Ancient Masters.

The Ancient Secrets give us the knowledge and understanding that all visions are real. The Manifestations of these visions are only reflections in the plane of existence. These Visions are molds with an irresistible power of attraction to draw and be filled with the cosmic substance; the stuff with which the entire Universe is made. Everything. Stars, galaxies, grains of sand, and the human body are all made with this one thing by adaptation.

This one thing, this cosmic substance with which the entire Universe is made, is Consciousness. Science calls this force Energy, and the Ancient Teachings call it Consciousness. The New Physics declares Consciousness creates reality. The *Vedas* and the *Bible* affirmed millenniums ago that Consciousness creates reality,

> *Consciousness is the Creator*
>
> - Rg Veda, Aitareya Upanishad 3.3

> *All things were made by him; and without him was not any thing made that was made.*
>
> - John 1:3

Substance of Creation

All substance is Consciousness. It is the substance with which everything is made and with which everything operates. It is perfect harmony. It is the power that is pumping your lungs right now and the power with which your heart is beating this very moment. It is the power with which you are reading these words and converting them to your understanding. You live and move and have your Being in this substance. It is all knowing and it fills the molds of your visions and manifests them.

As Jesus of Nazareth said, “I do nothing of myself: The Father that dwelleth in me, He doeth the works.”

When you use this power to make your visions a reality you don’t do anything, you see it being done. You are an observer who watches it all unfold with detachment. This is a key premise of the Ancient Secrets and it is repeated in the teachings of traditions throughout history.

Not doing anything will be difficult because you have been conditioned to working and toiling for everything that you had desired in the past. You can overcome this difficulty by returning to your origin, to your true Being, and entering the Absolute through meditations as given in Part Two. These meditations have been tested through millenniums and are the fountain of the elixir of life. You will enter a place in your heart that is prior to Manifestation, prior to conditions, and Unlimited.

Not doing anything doesn't mean being indolent and idle. On the contrary you will be engaged in more activity than before; with a difference, that is, all your activity will be accomplished with serenity and calmness and your work will be a joy. You will need to carry on your present work with the knowledge that what you have visioned is certain to manifest as you see it in your mind's eye. All the necessary connections and resources will be attracted to you. All the ways and means that you will require to fulfill your vision will find their way to you. In modern day parlance and in Science it is called Synchronicity. The whole Universe is perfectly synchronized.

When these connections and resources are presented to you, you must act on them; not with excitement or undue haste, for you know you can't make a mistake as your goal is already accomplished. There are no accidents in this world and all seeming accidents can be analyzed to show that they were not accidents but an unfolding of a vision.

At the moment, your Consciousness is trapped in your present conditions. Your ability to discriminate or judge is shackled by your present sensations. Your expectations are imprisoned by your past experiences. The Ancient Secrets smash these shackles to smithereens and break open the prison doors that have held you captive and will set you free to create a life of your own design.

Transmitting Wisdom

Knowledge can be transferred but wisdom can only be transmitted. The fire of meditation will burn the manure of all your past conditioning and the Universe will transmit the wisdom into your heart; that you are Invincible and Omnipotent and that you are made in the image and likeness of God. You are the Creator. Immersed in this wisdom you will become still and know that you are the *I Am That I Am*. Only then will you be able to hold a vision created by you in the Absolute and manifest it as per the instructions of the great Master, Jesus of Nazareth. Listen to him,

> *Therefore I say unto you, what things so ever ye desire, when ye pray, believe that ye receive them, and ye shall have them.*
>
> - Mark 11:24

Then finally you will be able to understand the import of the great dictum, "Ask and Receive."

Your belief will become your knowing. You will become detached to everything that you desire, which means you will not be anxious as to how your desire is going to be fulfilled, you will not be concerned about the future, you will live with certainty. Detachment does not in any way indicate your aloofness towards your desire but to the contrary it reveals to you that you have total reliance on the Universe to bring to you what you want.

Detachment allows this intelligent cosmic substance to organize itself with perfection to bring you your vision in space and time, if you only let it. Do not superimpose your vision of what you want with images of failure that are created by anxiety and concern of the future. Detachment in no way indicates your lack of interest or being unconcerned about results. It confirms that you know the Ancient Secrets of Success; whatever you want, you will have.

Two Creations

There are always two creations; one in your heart and the other in time and space. The creation in time and space is impossible if it is not first created in your heart, which is your Consciousness. The Ancient Wisdom of Solomon reconfirms the same, “For as [a man] thinketh in his heart, so is he." (Proverbs 23:7)

The whole Universe works in perfect harmony and is perfectly synchronized. Synchronicity is the very basis of creation. The Masters of the past and present trust it implicitly. They give it names such as Faith, Understanding, and Self Reliance. For every Vision, the Universe organizes and harmonizes ways to manifest it into time and space. Every time you develop a vision the Universe commands all its infinite resources to manifest your vision. Every Vision develops its own laws in harmony with the Universe to bring it into manifestation without fail.

Your Vision is already in your heart, your Consciousness, the Absolute where there is no time and space. This is the first creation. And it will unfailingly reflect in the mirror of existence, which is in the manifested world of the senses, the inevitable second creation. When you know this you will not in any way shape or form be concerned about the process of the second creation. That is the secret of the power of detachment.

Just hold the vision. Be still and know that it is already accomplished and hurtling down to you to be experienced by your five senses. Your heart has already experienced it. If your heart has not experienced it, it will not manifest and be experienced by your five senses. Do not waver.

Using the Ancient Secrets will prevent you from wavering, from having attacks of doubt, disbelief, and possible anxiety. Sometimes these arch enemies, doubt, fear and anxiety, will overwhelm you. You must not give up. You must practice the Secrets assiduously, continuously, and persistently and you must meditate while conducting your daily life at work, at home, and while playing with your children and going out on a date with your spouse. Every breath of yours glorifies the Supreme that dwells in your heart and is the Substance and Being of everything.

You cannot give up. What is left for you if you do? You must practice. And it will become as natural to you as your breath is. You will become as detached to the manifestation of your vision as you are to your next breath.

The Four Steps to Visioning and Manifesting Your Vision

You will be shown how your vision goes through four steps as it manifests. These four steps don't happen as your intellect expects they would. You will experience conscious control of your Vision. These Four Steps do not take place sequentially but are an at-onceness.

Whether you are aware of it or not, this process is operating in your world this very moment and has brought you everything that is in your life today. By knowing and applying the Four Steps to Visioning and Manifesting Your Vision, you can take control of your life.

Having the knowledge and the wisdom of the Secrets gives you power over your circumstances. You become the Master of your life, the commander of your mind. You live in constant bliss, transcending pain and pleasure and all the pairs of opposites.

The Ancient Secrets assure more than just success. They give more than a sure-fire method of setting and manifesting goals. They give you back control of your life so that you Master it. That is true success, a process done in perfect bliss and without exertion.

Unlike the poor storekeeper in the story of the Touchstone who bargained with life, you become the Master of your life.

The Antidote for Anxiety and Doubt

Anxiety and doubt are the viruses which disintegrate your Vision before it even gets a chance to be firmly formed in your mind. Anxiety and doubt are like parasites that suck out all the marrow of life. When they get a grip on us, they paralyze our ability to think creatively. We cannot think the thoughts that we want to think. We only permit ourselves to dwell on thoughts that keep on perpetuating our anxiety and doubt. This is what we call worry. The memory bank crashes. Our feelings and all our senses become numb.

We seem to have become accustomed to living with worry. We don't notice our anxiety and doubt most of the time. We seem to have accepted it as a part of our daily life. We don't realize that we have enrolled in the biggest club of the world; the club of doubters, which governs our life.

That is why it is our responsibility to ask, what causes anxiety and doubt and worry? How do we uproot these monsters from our life? Anxiety and doubt are the cause of all our problems in life. The answer to these two questions is the heart of *Ancient Secrets of Success*.

The cause of anxiety and doubt is in our exclusive reliance on the mind which can only depend on past experiences and memories. It cannot see the future. It can only anticipate the future and this anticipation is laced with the poison of anxiety and doubt. The mind lives in the past and anticipates the future. Consciousness does not live in the past, the present, or the future. Consciousness is the Absolute. Thought emerges from Consciousness and incubates in the mind. Thoughts do not belong in time and space. The mind makes thought a prisoner of time and space.

When a thought emerges from your Consciousness the mind becomes the moderator of the thought. Prior to thought is feeling. Feeling is the basis of thought. These feelings are modified by your mind before you are allowed to accept these feelings. Anxiety is a feeling of not being able to accomplish your objectives. This is worry.

What is worry? Worry is nothing else but another vision of what you expect will happen to you. A worry does not live in the past or the present or in the future. It is. Worry is just another vision. The great Master Jesus of Nazareth's prescription for demolishing worry fills his teachings. His instructions are,

> *And he said unto his disciples, Therefore I say unto you, Take no thought for your life, what ye shall eat; neither for the body, what ye shall put on.*

- Luke 12:22

He continues to emphasize not to rely on your mind for your provisions for your life but to rely completely on your Consciousness,

> *And which of you with taking thought can add to his stature one cubit? If ye then be not able to do that thing which is least, why take ye thought for the rest? Consider the lilies how they grow: they toil not, they spin not; and yet I say unto you, that Solomon in all his glory was not arrayed like one of these.*
>
> - Luke 12:25-27

Transferring the Reliance

Ancient Secrets of Success gives you the insight of how you can take your current reliance from the mind to completely rely on your Consciousness. And give the mind its rightful place to serve you and not to be served by you.

Every thought is physical action. Thinking takes as much physical labor as it would to build a piece of furniture. Mental exhaustion is more intense than physical exhaustion. Worry exhausts the individual and renders him powerless to face the day to day duties of life. The dictum of the Masters of the Ancient Traditions is to Vision and not to worry about how you are going to see the Vision manifested in your life. Your duty is to hold the vision and have complete reliance on your Consciousness to bring to you all the circumstances, and ways, and means necessary to manifest it.

To worry about the fruits of action indicates your lack of trust in your Consciousness. The energy expended in worry drains away the energy to build a Vision. It exhausts your ability to create what you want.

Your Consciousness is all powerful. All the power of the Universe, past, present and future, the power that created the sky, the earth, the galaxies, a grain of sand, a flower – is in you at this very moment. You don't need to go anywhere else for your building materials or the workforce to build your vision. You already have it.

When you are concerned about the fruits of your actions, of how your vision will manifest, you build a second vision on top of the original one. But this second vision paints a picture, showing how you won't get what you want, and how you won't receive what you originally asked for. This new picture overpowers the first one and erases it before your original vision even had a chance to take shape.

To be concerned about the future, to be anxious about the process of how your vision is going to manifest, is creating an intention to fail. This is called attachment. You cannot figure the process out. Your mind can only see the past.

If your Consciousness can vision it, you must know that Consciousness at the same time knows how to manifest it. Your job at this point is to stay out of the way of the Universe to bring your vision into manifestation. You need to carry on with your present work diligently with the full assurance that you will get what you have visioned. Expect it as you would expect the sun to rise tomorrow. It is not make-believe, because you know the reasons why you will have it. *Ancient Secrets of Success* gives you the tools to live in this state of Consciousness.

You will be given meditations that will free your mind from your attachment to the process. You will know the Infinitude of Consciousness. You will be given the insight into the essence of the Ancient Secrets through Four Proclamations which have parallels in Ancient Teachings across the world.

Your desire will manifest if you stay detached to the process; allow the Infinite Universe, which is individualized in you, to find the ways and means to bring you what you desire. It will happen because your Consciousness already has it. Your Consciousness does not live in time and space. You are Consciousness.

We are at this moment not fully reliant on Consciousness. We cannot rely on our Consciousness partially. We must rely on our Consciousness completely or not at all. Most of the time, we rely on our circumstances, conditions, and past experiences. Abundance and joy is our inheritance. Now we must reclaim our heritage by relying totally on Consciousness, the cause of everything moving and unmoving.

The veil over your Divinity will be rent apart with the meditation on the Four Proclamations and will cleanse your heart of doubt, fear and anxiety. You will learn to trust your Consciousness implicitly to manifest your vision.

The following story has been told a thousand times by Masters throughout the ages to reveal to us our state of mind before we knew the world of the Absolute and the Unconditioned. This story will be in your memory bank to guide you through when the virus of doubt and anxiety raises its ugly head.

CHAPTER 5

THE STORY OF THE FROG OF THE WELL AND THE FROG OF THE OCEAN

How We Form Limitations and Break Free From Limitations

Once upon a time a crane caught a frog from the ocean and was taking it to its babies for dinner. As the crane was flying over a well, the frog struggled out of the beak of the crane and fell into the well. It was a shocker for the frog of the ocean when he plunged into the deep well.

After he recovered and came to his senses he saw that a strange frog, sitting on a floating log of wood, was staring at him. The frog of the well asked him, "Where did you come from?"

"From the Ocean," said the frog of the Ocean.

"How big is the Ocean?" asked the frog of the well.

The frog of the Ocean did not want to tell him the size of the Ocean, as he felt that the frog of the well would not be able to understand the immensity of his world. He just kept silent.

The frog of the well thought that either the frog of the Ocean was suffering from a shock from the plunge he took or he was shocked at the size of his huge well. The frog of the well had never ever seen any other place in the Universe. The little well was his world. For him nothing else could be bigger. That was his belief.

So he said to the frog of the Ocean, "Look! Make yourself comfortable; there is plenty of room here just on this log of wood. You take the other end, and I will continue to live where I am living."

The frog of the Ocean thanked him and took up his new residence.

The frog of the well couldn't help himself and his curiosity got the better of him. He asked, "Tell me how big is this place that you come from? Is it half the size of this well?" He was sarcastic and was trying to be painfully funny.

The frog of the Ocean still kept silent. He knew that it was not possible to make the frog of the well believe that there were other worlds, and that they were far too big for his comprehension. He also knew that if he did tell him, he would not be able to prove it to him as there was no way out of this little well, the world of this little frog. He could not take him to the Ocean.

The frog of the well would not give up. He insisted on finding out from the frog of the Ocean the size of his world and kept on asking him.

Finally one day the frog of the Ocean, caught off guard by the frog of the well, broke his silence and said, "The Ocean is infinite. If all the wells like this one were put in the Ocean they would get lost in the Ocean." After saying this, the frog of the Ocean realized that he had broken his silence and made himself stand foolish in front of ignorance.

The frog of the well did not know whether to laugh or to cry that he now was destined to live with a raving mad frog. He humored the frog of the Ocean and mourned for himself.

He said to the frog of the Ocean, "Don't worry, everything will be okay for you; once the shock of the plunge you took into the well…right from the jaws of death…has worn off."

The frog of the Ocean returned to his silence. The frog of the well started to take care of the frog of the Ocean and expected to heal him of his mental disorder.

It so happened that in that region there was a big ferocious flood and all the wells overflowed. The two frogs found themselves out of the well. The frog of the Ocean knew his way home to the Ocean. He took his forced companion, the frog of the well, and showed him the Ocean.

The frog of the well saw a new world. His mind expanded and became the Ocean. He too became silent.

CHAPTER 6

THE EVERYDAY MAGIC OF CREATING FROM NO-THING

The Substance of Your Personal Creative Power That Gets You What You Want

Without exception, whether we realize it or not, creation is always from No-Thing. That is how all existence has come; out of No-Thing. That is how the Universe was created; out of No-Thing. Success is assured when this fact becomes your belief system. This is the Truth which the Masters of Antiquity taught their students.

The human mind refuses to acknowledge this fact that all things are made of No-Thing; like the frog of the well could not believe that any place could be bigger than his little well. His beliefs only affect his own little world. The Ocean will still be there whether the frog of the well believes it or not, and your and my belief will not change the creative process of the Universe. It is true nonetheless that matter is No-Thing. It is not a matter of conjecture or speculation anymore; we know that matter reduced to its ultimate stage is energy and No-Thing.

In the allegories of creation we see that substance is created out of Consciousness. That your Consciousness and Universal Consciousness are identical. That Consciousness is No-Thing. That Consciousness is the Creator and also the substance with which creation is manifested. Your thought is Consciousness and your thought has made your world. Every thing and every condition and all the people that you have around you have been brought to you by your Consciousness, by your thought.

A Single Thought Can Change Your World

A single thought can change your world at this very moment. The very thought that you create out of No-Thing is true, and if you allow it to dwell in your heart your world will change now. You will see the Ocean. If you cannot, know that the meditations of the Ancient Masters, in Part Two of *Ancient Secrets of Success*, will lead you to the Truth of your very Being.

The biggest stumbling block for a successful life is dependency on conditions. That is, dependency on your circumstances. You say, "If I had these conditions of wealth and connections I would be able to achieve this goal." In this scenario you are making the accomplishment of your goal dependent on certain specific conditions. You don't have at this time all the knowledge that you need to accomplish what you want. You have become dependent not only to the substance that you want but also to your past experience.

This is putting the cart before the horse. The creative process is the polar opposite. You see what you want and see it being done and all the conditions to fulfill the desire will come at the right time and in the right way. The former way of setting a vision, which is relying on conditions, becomes an endless struggle and generates more thoughts of dependency on substance. This is what the Masters call limitations.

The Great Master, Jesus of Nazareth, with pristine clarity drew a picture of visioning and seeing the vision already fulfilled without depending on any conditions. He used a metaphor that boggles the intellect. He told his disciples,

> *"Say not ye, There are yet four months, and then cometh harvest? behold, I say unto you, Lift up your eyes, and look on the fields; for they are white already to harvest."*
>
> - John 4:35

The Master takes the natural phenomenon of farming as the metaphor. Everyone knows that it takes four months for the crop to grow provided all conditions of cultivation such as irrigation, the weather, and all other requirements are fulfilled. He tells his listeners to see the harvest at the same time as the seed is planted. This idea would have certainly raised a few eyebrows at that time. The fruit is in the seed and the seed is in the fruit. It will be well to contemplate on this metaphor and then you will know the secret of success is the secret of creation out of No-Thing.

The mind is prone to construction and not creation. Creation is out of No-Thing. No pre-existing condition is needed to create. On the other hand Construction must have pre-existing conditions. Construction is putting things together to build something. Construction is assembling parts and materials together. We are so used to constructing we become doubtful about our power to create from No-Thing.

The mind believes, "Nothing can come from nothing," and it takes root in our belief system. This is how most of us live out our lives. We swim against the current, which is our present conditions, to reach our goal. In this odyssey of swimming upstream in the river of life we become exhausted, tired and hopeless. And if we do reach to a facsimile of our goal we are too worn out to enjoy it.

To train the mind to believe that we create out of No-Thing is our mission in life. We must face the trials, tribulations, and seeming challenges of our daily existence with the knowledge that we create from No-thing and we require no pre-existing materials to manifest our desires. The challenges that besiege us are gifts though they appear troublesome. Each time we overcome them we come closer to our real Self, our Consciousness, and come closer to the idea that Consciousness produces the circumstances and the materials required to meet and overcome the challenges. Each time we accomplish a Vision by creation, we become more aware of who we really are; we also become more confident of our Divinity.

We must again and again witness our actions and apply the wisdom that we create our world and our circumstances out of No-Thing with our thoughts. We must continuously dwell in this wisdom till it becomes our natural way of thinking and feeling.

A materialist depends on materials and a Spiritualist depends upon Spirit. A Spiritualist knows that Spirit creates out of No-Thing.

A materialist depends on the past, the present, and the future. These three time zones are the source of all limitations. If inventors had depended on the past we would not have gone to the moon or have developed the Internet because neither seemed possible before. We would still be living very primitively. The metaphor of the harvest annihilates time and space. The Master tells his listeners to see the harvest not subject to time and space.

Inventors don't depend on the past. They overcome the limitations of the past to create what has never been created before and do what has never been done before.

Consciousness does not live in the past, the present, or the future. It does not understand time and space. It is. It was never born and it will never die. Consciousness is you and Consciousness is me. There was never a time that you were not and there will never be a time that you will cease to be. That is the feeling of Consciousness.

Life is thinking and feeling. Feeling creates thought and thought creates a mold which the Universe works to fill instantaneously. It pours the Universal Substance into the mold of thought to manifest it. That is why Science today declares we create by observation. Consciousness creates reality. The Universe is observer created.

The following story of the Scorpion and the Frog gives us a vivid picture of how our dependency on conditions has become our instinct. How we helplessly give in to our instincts and sabotage our own visions.

CHAPTER 7

THE STORY OF THE SCORPION AND THE FROG

How We Sting Success When it Stares Us in the Face

On a bank of a river lived a Scorpion and a Frog. The Scorpion wanted to cross the river. He could not swim. He asked the Frog to give him a ride on his back and take him to the other bank.

Thc Frog instinctively said, “I would love to help you out. But you see I can’t, because you see when I put you on my back you will sting me and I will die.”

The Scorpion laughed and replied, “Don’t be silly. Don’t you have any sense? I am smart and I also want to live. If I sting you and you die, I will drown and die too. You know that I can’t swim.”

The Frog was convinced. He took the Scorpion on his back and started to swim towards the other side of the river. As they came to the middle of the river the Scorpion forgot his purpose because his instincts overpowered him. He forgot about his own safety. His urge to sting started to intensify, and he was aching to sting. He could not help himself. He forgot about his goal to cross the river. He lost control over himself and stung the Frog.

The Frog looked up and said, “What did you do? Why did you sting me? Don’t you realize that now we are both going to die?”

The Scorpion replied, “I lost control. My habit had the better of me but I know that it is too late now.”

The Frog and the Scorpion died.

The Scorpion is our mind and intellect, and the Frog is our Consciousness. Our Consciousness creates and takes us to the goal set by the mind and intellect. The same mind and intellect sabotages the process with the sting of negative thoughts, thoughts of dependency on conditions and circumstances. We don’t seem to let our Consciousness take us to our destination.

The Masters knew the sting of the Scorpion was fatal to the Scorpion itself. They formulated a system with which the Scorpion can control his instincts and cross the river. Part Two will lead the reader through this process of controlling the sting of negative thoughts.

CHAPTER 8

WHY CAN'T WE HOLD A VISION AND MANIFEST THE VISION

If one man conquers in battle a thousand men a thousand times, and if another conquers himself, he, the latter is the greater conqueror.
- Gautama Buddha, Dhammapada, verse 103

We now know that we are Consciousness and Consciousness creates everything out of No-Thing. Then why don't we create the things we want to create? We know that we create by visioning, then why can't we hold a vision and manifest the Vision?

When our reliance is on circumstances and on our present conditions, the mind cannot believe that a Vision can physically materialize out of No-Thing. The reason we can't hold on to a Vision is because either we don't want it badly enough or we don't believe that visioning alone will get for us what we want.

We cannot hold on to a Vision that we cannot believe in. We cannot concentrate on a lie. You cannot forcibly picture yourself as a millionaire or whatever you want to be and keep on repeating like a parrot that you are a millionaire and become one, if you cannot fully rely on your Consciousness. A Vision can only be a Creative Vision if our mind agrees to believe in it. To train the mind to know the Truth, that Consciousness creates everything out of No-Thing, and that everything is made of and made with Consciousness, is the Secret of Success.

Are We In Control Of Our Mind?

Nothing affects us more than our mind. When we are in control of our mind we are in control of our life. Are we in control of our mind as much as we would like to be? How do we control our mind? The Ancient Masters have one answer; by continuous practice and detachment to the process of creation. The Masters say that just because your Consciousness has been awakened it does not mean a thing if you don't have control over your mind. All limitations are of the mind and all freedom is of the mind. The mind is like a white piece of cloth, whatever color you dip it in, it becomes that color.

Our Individuality is made up of Consciousness, body, mind, intellect, and the senses. The body, mind, intellect, and the senses are the equipment of Consciousness to take you to your destination. The *Katha Upanishad* of the *Vedas* draws a vivid picture of our Individuality. It says that Consciousness is the rider or the passenger in the chariot, which is the body. The intellect is the driver of the Chariot. The bridle or the reins which guide the horses is the mind, and the horses are the senses.

The Mind has a Thousand Eyes

Your Consciousness must take command and control of your mind. The mind is the instrument through which you create your world. The mind wants to take over and control your Consciousness. The mind cannot see beyond this moment. It does not allow Consciousness to Vision what it cannot understand. The mind has a thousand eyes and it cannot stay focused. The mind thinks that it is all that there is and denies the power of Consciousness which is the very foundation of the mind.

The mind is like a dog; it is loyal but it is not focused. It needs to be on a short leash and handled by Consciousness. A deeper look at this analogy would be that the dog, which is akin to our mind, is taking the Master, which is our Consciousness, for a walk on a leash instead of the Master taking the dog or the mind for a walk. This picture as ridiculous as it may look is what is happening in most of our lives today. The Secret of Success is to train the mind to obey the Master, which is our Consciousness.

No amount of theory can train the mind. You cannot learn to swim by reading a book on swimming no matter how great a book it may be. You will have to enter the water and learn by practice. It is the same with training the mind to obey your command. It can only be done by practice, continuous practice. The process and the method of practice to train the mind to follow your command can be easily achieved by following the practice as given in Part Two of *Ancient Secrets of Success*. These practices and methods have been tested and tried for thousands of years very successfully. It is ageless and works without fail. If you work it.

When you cannot command your mind and your mind becomes

out of control that is when anxiety and depression raise their ugly heads. Sometimes you feel that insanity has got a grip on you. Insanity is one of the most painful diseases known to mankind. There is no pain more painful than mental pain.

The Ancients knew that no amount of theory would give you control of your mind. They also were certain that your mind is a physical instrument through which your Consciousness experiences the world of time and space. They knew that to experience this existence successfully and feel the ecstasy of life you must have full control over your mind.

The Ancient teachings and traditions have this one aim, to control the mind. The *Vedas* of India give step by step instructions of how you can practice and achieve control of your mind. In Part Two of *Ancient Secrets of Success* this practice has been distilled and presented to you so that you can take charge of your own life.

The Mind is like a Scorpion

The mind is like the Scorpion and it wants to go to the other side. That is the Vision of the Scorpion. It can't swim, that is, it can't create. Only our Consciousness creates; only the Frog can swim and take the Scorpion to its Vision. What happens then? The Scorpion can't wait because it has no control over its tendencies, and before you know, it aborts the Vision with its instinctive sting. Its reliance is on the external conditions.

The body, mind, and the intellect are the equipment of Consciousness. The mind is a part of the body, it is physical. The mind is a memory bank of all your past. When the body is hungry and tired the mind cannot remember, just like the body becomes incapable of physical action. Then when the body is fed and nourished the mind becomes alert and it regains its memory, just like the body becomes capable of physical action again.

When you eat, the food is broken up by your digestive system and divided into three parts. The first part becomes excrement, the second part becomes blood and flesh, and the third part, which is the subtle part of the food, becomes the mind. The quality of your diet has an effect on your mind.

The Mind is the Subtle Body

The mind is your subtle body. This is not a so-called spiritual explanation; ask any medical practitioner, he will tell you that there is a subtle body. When a person's arm or leg is amputated his amputated limb still itches and he even feels the pain in that limb which is not there, at least not visible. The mind is not Consciousness. It is a part of the body.

The mind can be altered with food and drugs because it is physical. Your Consciousness is not your mind. It is the urge in you to experience Bliss which transcends happiness. You get glimpses of it in moments of your life. These moments become frozen in your mind. Moments like when you hold your baby for the first time in your arms or when you are engulfed in a romantic embrace or when you get immersed in the glory of a sunrise against the mountains.

The Mind is the Memory of All Your Past

The mind feels. Your mind is the memory of all your past. Your memory develops your tendencies which we call our 'mindset.' The intellect is the decision maker. It is the driver of the body. The mind feels that it is all that is. It does not want to acknowledge Consciousness. Consciousness is the thinker and the mind is the feeler. Consciousness Visions and the mind feels the reality of the Vision only when it can relate it to the past. If it doesn't have any reference point in the past it immediately rejects the Vision of Consciousness and relegates it to the realm of fantasy or dream. This is the sting of the Scorpion.

The Mind cannot see the future. The mind can only compute the future on the basis of past feelings and experiences. Then the mind recycles the garbage of the past to create the dread of the future. That is why the mind is frightened of the future. All its expectations of the future are based on past feelings and experiences. It cannot create new Visions. It is chained to the past.

The senses are the equipment of the mind. Our senses are like wild horses and our mind is like the bridle to keep the senses on its track.

The *Bhagavad-Gita* says,

> *That the senses are turbulent and violently snatch away the mind of even the wise man, striving after perfection.*
>
> *For the mind that follows the wake of the senses, carries away his discrimination, as a wind carries off its course a boat on the waters.*
>
> - Bhagavad-Gita Chapter 2 verses 60 and 67

Consciousness is the only creative power of the Universe. If you are not conscious of a thing, the thing does not exist for you. The mind does not create. Consciousness creates. The mind facilitates or moderates the thoughts of Consciousness in line with its tendencies. For example, your Consciousness wants to travel around the world or be a millionaire while you are currently in deep debt; your mind will moderate your thinking of traveling or being rich and will not allow you to entertain that Vision. Your indebtedness becomes your tendency. In this scenario you have restricted your Consciousness to your mindset. You have allowed your mind to usurp your creative power by your mind's present state of feeling.

You are Consciousness. The mind, body, and intellect are your equipment. You have lowered your Self by becoming the slave of the mind. You just stung the Frog before you could even start the journey.

The following illustration may further paint a vivid picture of your constant reliance on the mind and not on your Consciousness. Every time I go to the ocean I practice this as a form of meditation in training the mind.

I can hardly swim but my Consciousness knows that if I lie on my back on the water, my body will float. I will not sink. Yet when I lie on the water my senses tell me that I will drown. After a second or two I start relying on the senses. I struggle against the water, trying to use my hands and legs to stay afloat. I give in to the slavery of the mind and lo and behold....I sink. My mind makes me believe that the water can't hold my body up as the senses find that liquid cannot hold up a solid.

How many have drowned struggling against the water? All they have to do is to let go and lie on the water. When a person drowns and dies his body floats. The body weight has not decreased. All he had to do is let go and let the water hold him up.

One day I decided that no matter what, I will lie on the water and look up at the blue sky and feel that the Universe is holding me up in her lap. No matter how many waves come over me I will lie still on the water. It was ecstasy when the first gentle wave came towards me and I lay still. The wave lifted me up and gently gave me a floating ride towards the shore. I lay still and the waves came frolicking to play with me and gently carried me onto the warm beach. I had a realization of how we struggle against our own Being, our Consciousness, and surrender to the mind's little world of past memories.

Your Vision of being rich and traveling around the world when you are in deep debt is not any different. It is as the Ancient Masters called it an inner urge, the urge of Consciousness; the urge of your Consciousness to experience what you have not experienced before. This urge is the child of your Consciousness and the mind is the midwife. The midwife must be trained to help give birth to your inner urge which defies all logic. Just remember your body is a perfect feat of creation, a challenge to Science and Engineering, and was made without hands and feet. Your very existence defies logic. The mind cannot understand any of this. And if you ask the mind how your body was made without hands and feet it will get bewildered.

If all the Visionaries of the world were bound by the turbulent senses and the mind, whose reference point is the past, then we would not be flying across the world faster than sound. We would not be able to communicate with each other across the globe and from the moon instantaneously. We would still be living in the dark ages.

Consciousness does not get caught up with circumstances and conditions. Consciousness easily transcends all adverse circumstances, not by changing the present conditions, but by creating a new Vision. We must train the mind to obey Consciousness, every command of Consciousness.

Never forget to watch your mind. And watch how your mind is modifying your Consciousness to fit the mind's memory and circumstances. Be on guard and take immediate corrective measures, and if need be, be paranoid about it. You have nothing to lose and everything to gain. The final instruction the Lord gives to the Great General who buckled under at the sight of his enemy in the *Bhagavad-Gita,* is to abandon all his tendencies and his entire intellectual prowess and offer his mind to Consciousness. He tells the General that Consciousness will liberate him from all limitations and he will become fearless. You too must offer your mind to Consciousness and live in fearlessness.

Taming the Tiger in the Mind

How do we offer our mind to Consciousness when we don't have control over it? It is like telling a wild, ferocious, man-eating Royal Bengal Tiger to train itself for performing in the Circus. All the training will have to be processed through the mind to train the mind. In view of this the Ancients formulated a system of meditation, accompanied by knowledge, which will bypass the mind and train the mind to renew itself. Then the mind will mold and hold the Vision of your Consciousness without argument. This is the Secret of Success. This will be further explained in Part Two of *Ancient Secrets of Success*.

The mind must have a clear understanding of the operation of Consciousness and the process of creation from No-Thing. The mind also needs to know the difference between the Absolute and the Relative and how the Relative is created from the Absolute. To prepare you to understand the Absolute and the Relative, Consciousness and matter, Chapter 10 gives a graphic explanation which the mind can relate to easily. This is a form of external meditation through the instrument of symbols. It is both theory and meditation.

Wrestling with the mind is the most exhausting action that we can engage in. These symbols are like emergency tools to neutralize the mind's grip on a false reality. These symbols will help you to take control of the turbulent mind and put it on a short leash. And then it will enable you to think the thoughts that your Consciousness wants to think.

We must at all times work on renewing the mind and not conform to our old ways. As St. Paul in his Epistle to the Romans writes, "And be not conformed to this world: but be ye transformed by the renewing of your mind...." (Romans 12:2)

Messenger of Consciousness

Your mind is the messenger of Consciousness. Your present state of mind tries to interpret and translate the message in accordance with the tendencies of the mind. Through meditation and practice, your mind will become fully transparent and carry the message of Consciousness without any distortion and manifest what your Consciousness wants.

Be on guard and be alert; watch your mind as you would your

most prized possession. A great Roman, Cicero said, "The price of liberty is eternal vigilance."

The following story illustrates that our Consciousness is a Wish Fulfilling Tree and we are sitting under the shade of this magnificent tree. Everything we wish for appears to us only if we don't interfere with its workings. Our interference is our counter suggestions that our Consciousness is incapable of fulfilling our Vision. They deny the Infinite power of Consciousness. We overlook the greatest power, the power of Infinitude. Do we really know what Infinitude is when we say or write the word 'Infinite?' Consciousness is Infinite and beyond the grasp of the mind. Can the Infinite be incapable of fulfilling its Vision?

CHAPTER 9

THE STORY OF THE WISH FULFILLING TREE

How to Guard the Self-Sabotaging Mind

In a small village far away from anywhere and with no access road to the nearest town lived a poor Farmer. He had nobody. No family to help him to farm. He was all alone.

In the heat of a scorching summer's day he had to go to town to buy seeds for his next crop. He had to walk there while the sun beat down on the parched earth and on him. It was hot.

Halfway to town the Farmer saw a beautiful Tree with long and strong branches, still filled with green luscious leaves. Under the Tree at the base of the trunk it was cool and the shade defiantly challenged the scorching Sun. He decided to rest there for a while.

As he was dozing off in the cool of the shade resting under the Tree he thought if he would have a cold glass of water it would be great. He did not realize that he was sitting under a Wish Fulfilling Tree. Before you know it, he saw a very cold and refreshing glass of water before him. He quenched his thirst and wished if only he could have some sweets and some food. Lo and behold he saw a banquet before him.

After having had the meal of his life he wished, if only he would have a bed to take a nap. He was lying on a most comfortable bed before he could even speak his thought out completely. He immediately thought if only he had a house to sleep in on this comfortable bed and the house was there before you know it.

The fulfillment of one wish led to larger and larger wishes. Before you know, he had wanted the most beautiful woman for a wife and had plenty of children to help him in the farm, and there he was surrounded by family and wealth.

When he saw what he got just by wishing; he got a little worried. No, as a matter of fact he got a lot worried. He thought, “What will happen if now a ferocious man eating tiger comes out of the jungle and eats me up?”

A ferocious man eating tiger appeared and ate him up. He was still sitting under the Wish Fulfilling Tree.

We live and move and have our Being under the Wish Fulfilling Tree. This Tree is our Consciousness, the individualized Cosmic Consciousness. The same Power that created this magnificent Universe which cannot be comprehended by our mind, let alone by our brains. This Power works without question or pause and will not judge your wishes, it will fulfill them instantly.

Everything, every circumstance and every condition in your life whether in the past or in the moment was brought to you by your thoughts from this Wish Fulfilling Tree.

CHAPTER 10

CENTERING YOURSELF FOR SUCCESS

How We Create and Change Our Circumstances

We know from science that everything visible in this Universe has come out of the invisible, this includes our body. *In-Visible* means that which is visible inside. The Visible means when it is outside and your senses can see it, touch it, smell it, taste it and hear it. The visible is called the relative because it relates exactly to the In-Visible which is called the Absolute. Mathematically you cannot have the relative if there is no Absolute.

The mind does not want to acknowledge the Absolute because the untrained mind is totally dependent on the senses. The senses can not go to the region of the Absolute. The mind accepts what it can feel with its senses and lets the intellect decide whether it is true or not. Anything that the mind cannot feel with its senses, the mind considers that as hocus-pocus. This is when the mind becomes limited, it denies the Absolute. This is living in denial. The mind is caught up in the relative only. The mind relies solely on what it sees outside and what the senses can relate to.

The reliance of the mind on the relative or the outside does not change the fact that all visible things evolve out of the inside or the Absolute. The relative cannot exist without the Absolute. It is the law.

The Law of Cause and Effect

When the mind relies on the relative for creation then the relative in turn becomes the cause of the next cycle of creation and reproduces more of the relative. It creates more of what you already have. It re-produces more of the same. Nothing new is created. This is what is called being trapped in your past thoughts and not being able to think out of the box. It is living on the leftover thoughts of all your yesterdays forever into the future. This is living in the ripple effect of your past deeds. This is what the *Vedas* called the entrapment of Karma.

The release from the iron grip of Karma or from the world of effects is the Secret of Success. It is simple and easy to perform. It is living in the wisdom of Cause or Absolute. It is living from the Center and not from the circumference as you will experience now as you read on.

The relative must have an Absolute. Without an Absolute you cannot have a relative. There cannot be an outside without an Inside and there cannot be an Inside without an outside. We live all the time in two worlds, the Visible and the In-Visible. The visible is the effect and the In-Visible is the cause. The In-Visible is the Thought and the visible is the Thing.

In actuality, the visible and the In-Visible are not two worlds but One. Only for the purpose of study do we show it as two. The Thought and the Thing are One. The Thought is the Thing. The visible and the In-Visible are One. There cannot be a visible without the In-Visible.

This is the law of cause and effect. The law of cause and effect cannot be violated and will work without exception and automatically. If you plant a plum seed you will get a plum tree and you will not get a cherry tree. It is as simple as that.

In the seed is the tree, in the Absolute is the relative, and in the Cause is the effect. The Cause is your thought and the effect is the thing which your senses feel. When we see a tree we know that the tree is an effect of the seed. Our mind cannot fully acknowledge that this mighty tree could have been inside the seed. Only because we see the tree with our senses and we know how a tree grows do we agree with the idea that the tree was in the minute seed. The untrained mind has the tendency to rely on the outside exclusively to generate thought. That is the cause of all our limitations. Thought is the seed and the thing is the tree. Every thought is alive with the thing that it manifests.

A good analogy to graphically explain this phenomenon of the Absolute and the relative, the cause and the effect, is the circle. The circle is a symbol of Perfection and of Infinity. It has no beginning and no ending.

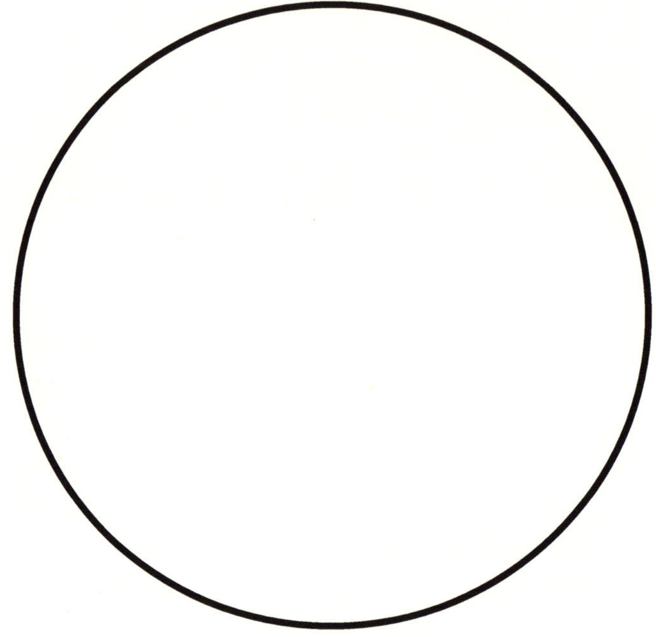

The visible circumference is a projection of the In-Visible center.

When we see a circle as shown here we only see the circumference. We know that every circle has a center and radius. A circle is made up of a center and circumference and the circumference is radiated from the center. This is why it is called radius because it radiates the center to the circumference. The center is invisible. The radius is also invisible; only the circumference is visible. Even if you put a dot at the center it does not make the center visible.

You will ask why? If you put a microscope over the dot which you marked as the center of the circle, you will see the dot as a jagged circle without a visible center. Then by using precision instruments and under a microscope if you do manage to put another dot in that smaller circle you still will not be able to see the center. If you put that dot under a still more powerful microscope you will again see another jagged circle. There is no end to this. You can take this process to infinity and you still cannot see the center. The center is the Absolute. It is In-Visible.

The center is the cause of the circumference. Without the center it is impossible to have a circumference. The center is thought and the circumference is the thing. The center generates the radius from itself to reproduce the circumference. In the same way, your thought will reach out to generate, with all the power that ever was or will be in the Universe, and radiate your thought into manifestation as seen by you in the center, your Absolute, your In-Visible world.

The circumference is your circum-stances in reference to your center, your Consciousness. Circumstances are the circumference of the center of the circle. You are the center and your circumstance is your circumference. Circum-stance means what you stand surrounded with.

Your circumstances should not make you; they only show you what you were. Your circumstances do not make you, you make your circumstances. If you want to change your circumstances all you have to do is to change the center, which is your thought and your vision of the conditions you want to have. Then by the unfailing law of cause and effect, you will have it. It works without fail.

You don't depend on your circumstances to make any changes. You have only to depend upon the Infinite power of your Consciousness, the center of your Being. Completely rely on your Consciousness which will radiate to you the conditions you desire.

Your circumstances do not make you. Your thoughts make you and your circumstances. Your thought is the center and your circumstance is the circumference. Where is your thought coming from? Is your thought coming from your Consciousness or is your thought coming from your circumstances?

Notice where your thought is coming from. If your thought is generated from your circumstance or the circumference, and then moving to your center or your Consciousness, then two major things are happening in your life.

First, you are reproducing more of the same circumstances you already have. The reason being, your thought is carrying the character of your present circumstances and conditions of your life. You are generating conditioned thought and not Absolute thought.

Your thought makes you what you are. You will produce more of the same condition.

Second, you are limiting your Consciousness to your present and past conditions. You are in essence denying yourself, your Consciousness, of its creative power. You become engaged in construction rather than creation. Your Consciousness creates. Your Consciousness now is relegated to labor with your circumstances instead of creating new conditions.

Two Kinds of Thought

In the *Amritabindu Upanishad* from the Vedic text, it says there are two kinds of thoughts, Unconditioned thought and Conditioned thought. Literally translated, it reads as Pure thought and Impure thought. Purity and Impurity in this context does not refer to morality or immorality. It defines the quality of thought, defined by the source of the thought. If the thought evolves out of conditions, past and present, it can only be conditioned thought. It is conditioned thought which the Ancients termed as impure thought; tainted by condition. Conditioned thoughts are generated from the senses and are driven by the senses.

Unconditioned thought or Pure thought is untainted by the senses; it is Unconditioned thought. Creative thought does not arise out of any conditions nor does it depend on any conditions to manifest the thought. An inventor usually has Unconditioned thought. Nothing is impossible to Unconditioned thought which arises from the Absolute.

When the mind is trained and our Consciousness is liberated from the senses, Unconditioned thought naturally arises. Consciousness becomes the Master of the mind and the senses. Mastery over the mind cannot be made with the mind. This is why the Ancients taught their students to transcend the mind through the realization of their Identity with Universal Consciousness. They realized Cosmic creation is an effect of Unconditioned thought and could not be generated out of Conditioned thought. There were no conditions to work with prior to Creation.

The Individual Consciousness is identical with Universal Consciousness just as a drop of the ocean has all the qualities of the ocean. The ocean is in the drop of the Ocean.

Unconditioned thought is beyond the reach of conditioned thought. Thinking from the Absolute and taking control over the mind can only be done by meditation on Consciousness. Milk is laced with butter but we can't see it. By churning milk the butter floats to the top and can never become milk again.

The Creative Process

The circle radiates from the center to the circumference and not from the circumference to the center. Life radiates from Consciousness to creation and not from creation to Consciousness. The center radiates the circumference with the projection of its radius from the center. Consciousness radiates the circumstances and conditions of your life with its Infinite radiant energy; the same radiant energy which is creating the physical Universe now.

The center of a circle, as we have seen earlier, has no dimension. It has no magnitude. It is the In-Visible out of which the visible circumference is radiated. The center is beyond time and space. It is Eternal and Everlasting. Free from limitations of time, from the past, present, and the future. Your Consciousness as the center of the circle has no dimension, nor magnitude. Your Consciousness is beyond time and space. It cannot think in the past nor think in the future and it is beyond the entrapment of the present.

The center of the Circle produces the circumference out of itself. The center is the stillness and there is no movement in the center. Out of this stillness radiates infinite movement to project the circumference. It is the same as a storm is projected from the eye of the storm where there is no movement. The eye of a storm is the center of the storm and it is perfect stillness. The raging storm moves and has its Being in the stillness of the eye of the storm. The Vision of the storm is in the eye of the storm.

Your Consciousness is the center of your world; it is perfect and it is stillness. Your Consciousness is your Being, your "I Am" and whatever you place after the "I Am" becomes your circumference, your circumstances. Your mind and your intellect cannot understand this Truth. Intellectually it is not possible to understand this concept.

How can the lesser understand the greater? How can a person living in a three dimensional world go to the people who live in a two dimensional world, a world where there is only length and width and no height, and try to explain to them about height. In the same way, the intellect is incapable of comprehending creation. It is only familiar with construction.

How can the finite understand the Infinite? Can the mind explain what is Infinite? Is it a stretching out to nowhere from somewhere? Is it growing bigger and bigger and on the reverse growing smaller and smaller limitlessly? The mind cannot explain it. Any point is finite. Any position is finite.

The Infinite is the Absolute and the Infinite is your Consciousness. Sometimes, in moments of bliss you may get a touch of Infinitude from the intoxication of Imagination; that is when your Imagination has climbed above the edge of conditions.

The Ancient Masters understood the plight of their students. They devised ways and means to make their students reach their Consciousness and live their life from the core of their Being; the center to the circumference and not the circumference to the center.

The Ancients from traditions across the world came out with parallel methods and they did not contradict each other in their process of training their students. These teachings came from opposite parts of the globe and still they were the same teachings.

The mind is like a dog. It loves its Master and will protect its Master at the cost of its own life. The dog needs to be trained. A dog without a leash can't stay focused. It sniffs everywhere and apparently without rhyme or reason. It barks at everything that it does not know or does not understand and often attacks any unknown entity coming its way. If the dog has no courage then instead of attacking, it runs away with its tail tucked between its legs.

The Ancients knew this difficulty of the mind and realized that in being protective of Consciousness it will attack or run from anything it does not understand. It will be unwilling to learn. It will resist any new knowledge or methods. The mind cannot stay focused and sniffs incessantly at everything that surrounds it unless it is held on a short leash by its Master, Consciousness. Setting the Vision from the mind is like asking the dog to set the vision of its own walk.

The Ancients through millenniums have perfected systems for making the mind realize that it does not do anything; Consciousness does everything. The mind facilitates Consciousness. Consciousness produces substance out of itself and creates. The mind and the intellect are incapable of understanding this as much as they are incapable of producing anything. Jesus of Nazareth said it beautifully, "But rather seek ye the kingdom of God; and all these things shall be added unto you." (Luke 12:31)

The Kingdom of God is the Absolute, beyond time and space and the center of your Being, the region of Unconditioned thought. In Unconditioned thought there is no doubt or anxiety, it is a certainty because there is no dependency on any condition to manifest the thought. It is a state of assured expectation. If there is any doubt then the thought has been lowered to the status of conditioned thought, impure thought. Then you have become dependent on some conditions to manifest your thought. It becomes construction and not creation.

Yoga of Manifestation

Prior to the manifestation of the circumference, the circumference was in the center of the Circle and was In-Visible. Prior to the manifestation of your vision, your vision is in your Consciousness, and it is In-Visible.

The oak tree is in the acorn but if you cut open the acorn you will not see the oak tree, not even a miniature form of the oak tree. It is

In-Visible. All the branches and the leaves of the oak tree are in the acorn. All the conditions of the manifestation of your Vision are in the Absolute and they are In-Visible.

Yoga means union culminating into Unity to become One with your aim or Vision. When you have a Vision, your Vision becomes your mark, your target. You become One with your target. This is what happens in your Consciousness when you want to manifest your Vision. You become one with your mark, your Vision. You become the Vision. The following example will give you a graphic picture of the Yoga of Visioning.

The Union of the Archer with the Mark

When the target, the bull's eye, the arrow, the pulled bow, and the archer become One then the archer releases the arrow. The target of an archer is the Intention. The arrow is the concentration of the intention into a Vision on the arrowhead. The bow is the mind and the archer is Consciousness. When the archer releases the arrow he does not doubt for a moment that he is going to hit the mark. If he did, he would not release the arrow. And if he does miss the mark he knows that his concentration and the steadiness of his mind with his Consciousness were not in perfect unity. He tries again. This is practice and this in Sanskrit is called *Sadhana*.

The *Bible* was translated from Greek. The word Sin in Greek is *Hamartia* which means missing the mark. That is when you set a mark or an Intention and you miss; you have sinned; you have missed the mark. So you have to try again; that is forgiving yourself. You will not gain forgiveness till you accomplish hitting the mark. This is the Yoga of holding a Vision and manifesting a Vision.

You can only forgive yourself by redeeming your mind and intellect from the clutches of Circumstances. To serve Consciousness you must have a mark and hit the mark. Anyone who truly loves himself will take on the responsibility of having a Vision for their life. You cannot have a life without a Vision. You cannot live in a vacuum. There is nowhere in the Universe a vacuum. Having no Vision is living in emptiness. The cause of all anxiety in life is a life without vision.

When you have a vision, you have a mark. If you do miss the mark you must assiduously practice hitting the mark till you do. If you don't hit the mark you will always carry the regret of missing the mark and that is living in hell, which is living in denial of your Infinitude.

You cannot ever miss the mark when you are One with your Consciousness; when you are living from the center to the circumference and not from the circumference to the center. It is impossible to miss the mark when you are living from the Absolute to the relative, from the Cause to the effect. *With God all things are possible. All things are possible to him that believeth.*

PART TWO

THE APPLICATIONS OF THE ANCIENT SECRETS OF SUCCESS

CHAPTER 11

THE PRACTICE OF THE ANCIENT SECRETS OF SUCCESS

The Essential Insights

To think out of the box, to be free from conditions, and to think the thoughts you want to think and manifest the thoughts is Success. The goal of life is to take command and control of thought. To think the thoughts you want to think regardless of your present and past conditions, is having Mastery over the mind.

You cannot take control of your mind with your mind. That is ridiculous. The Ancients devised a way to enter the subtle intelligence of your mind through a system of words and meditations. These meditations have withstood the scrutiny of the ages victoriously. These meditations are the instruments of your mind to develop a calm and tranquil mind without worry and anxiety.

The mind needs the confidence that Consciousness is Infinite and that Consciousness is All Power and All Wisdom; that the security of the mind is in Consciousness. The mind feels alone and helpless, and wants security and the mind cannot trust anything that it cannot understand. It is beyond the capacity of the mind to comprehend Infinite Consciousness.

The mind does not know that it is the Center of expression of the Infinite Power of the Universe. It is itself not the power; it is a center of expression of All Power. The only way the mind can know that it is the center through which the Universe creates is by experience.

This experience can only be gained from surrender to Consciousness with love. It is a surrender of Union. The mind and Consciousness have to become One. The Ancients called it the Mystical Marriage. Consciousness is the provider and the mind is the distributor, a parallel of the Ancient cultures where the husband is the provider and the wife is the distributor.

The Book of Revelation reveals this Union, this Mystical Marriage of Consciousness and mind eloquently,

> *And I saw a new heaven and a new earth: for the first heaven and the first earth were passed away; and there was no more sea. And I John saw the holy city, new Jerusalem, coming down from God out of heaven, prepared as a bride adorned for her husband.*
>
> - Revelation 21:1-2

A whole new Heaven and a whole new Earth is formed in our world when we enter in this Union. Our life becomes as calm as the depth of the ocean and the ripples above on the surface do not disturb the calmness within, in the depth. The old and troubled and limited world shall pass away. This is Yoga, this is Unity, and this is the concept of the Father and the Son becoming One. The Ancient Masters expressed this Union as a marriage and a loving relationship between a Father and Son.

This Union cannot be arrived at intellectually, as the lesser cannot comprehend the greater. This is the great impasse of the mind, to reach out and embrace Consciousness. The Ancient Masters with all their compassion understood and devised ways for the unsteady mind to first become steady, and then become still, and then realize its relationship with Consciousness, and then Unite and become Consciousness in total sweet surrender.

In the *Bhagavad-Gita* the Lord states that He is Consciousness, and He is the past, present, and the future. That Consciousness is omnipresent, which means, it is everywhere and everywhen. He also says that Consciousness is our destination, Consciousness is the witness, and Consciousness is our refuge, our friend, and our foundation. It is the destroyer of the old, the builder of the new, it is our home, our treasure house, and Consciousness is our seed or origin, which is imperishable.

The poetry of this Union of Consciousness and the mind is a hallmark in the *Vedas*. The mind invokes Consciousness and sings, "You are my Father and my Mother. You are my friend and my companion. You are all my knowledge and my wisdom. You are all the substance there is, and you are my everything, you are the Deity of all deities."

The meditations as taught by the Ancients give the mind the

belief system to trust that Consciousness is the Master and a loving Master. That Consciousness is the Creator and the substance of everything. That Consciousness is its individuality. That the mind is a center of expression of Consciousness. That your Individuality is not your mind; your Individuality is your individualized Consciousness. That you and Universal Consciousness are One. Your individual Consciousness is the same as Universal Consciousness. The spark of the blaze is the same as the blaze. Their size is irrelevant. The spark has all the power of the blaze to create the same blaze.

Knowledge to Wisdom

It is not possible through the medium of knowledge to liberate the mind from the entrapment of conditions and the mind's futile intellectual wrangling. As we stated earlier, knowledge can be transferred but wisdom cannot be transferred. Wisdom can only be transmitted. The meditations that you are about to enter into will transmit the wisdom into your mind and liberate you to think the thoughts that you want to think. This is knowing the Truth. And this Truth will set you free.

Part Two of *Ancient Secrets of Success* will lead you step by step in the process of meditation. You live from the center to the circumference. You will live from Consciousness to condition and not from condition to Consciousness. You will be guided through the process and then you will be given the Four Steps to Visioning and Manifesting the Vision. All this that you have gone through was just the preparation and now the journey begins.

CHAPTER 12

CROSSING OVER TO SUCCESS

Transcending Theory and Entering Wisdom

We have seen that Consciousness is the Intelligence and the Substance of everything in and around our life. We are Consciousness. For example when we say *I am happy* or *I am rich* or *I am in love,* we are expressing a state of our Consciousness. If we are not Conscious of a thing, that thing does not exist for us. Consciousness is our life. When we are unconscious we don't feel. Life is feeling.

The Ancients tell us that everything is made by Consciousness and with Consciousness. The substance we call matter is Consciousness. The New Physics confirms that Consciousness creates reality. What we observe is what we are conscious of. The

New Physics also says that the world is observer created. Your world is what you are observing. Everything that you will ever create will have to be observed by you before you can have it.

You are Consciousness. I am Consciousness. Our Individual Consciousness comes from Universal Consciousness. Where is our Individual Consciousness arising from? Why do we need to know? Our life is Consciousness. We need to know what Consciousness is and where it is arising from. If we don't know where our Consciousness is arising from we will be floating in the vast field of existence lost without direction and have no control over our life. We will not know how to live and why we live. If you don't know where you come from and who you are then how would you know where you want to go or where you can go? Isn't it madness to be oblivious about our Consciousness? There is an old story which illustrates this state of Consciousness.

The Story of the Lion Cub Who Was Raised by Goats

How We Deny Our Identity and Stay Ordinary

One day a hunter killed a lioness and dragged it away. He did not know that she had a cub in the cave, and left it there. The cub was helpless. There were some goats around who felt for the lion cub, and brought up this cub as one of their own.

The Lion cub grew up eating what the goats ate, it thought what the goats thought, it bleated as the goats bleated and it lived as a goat. It did not know anything better. It was happy and contented and scared of everything and survived on grass and leaves.

Then one glorious day a magnificent lion appeared on a hillock around where the goats were grazing and gave a loud roar. All the goats ran helter-skelter. The lion cub did not run. He felt a sense of kinship but did not know what it was. The cub looked up in amazement at this regal powerhouse, and stood still. The Lion walked up to the cub and said, "Who are you? Where is your mother? And why do you eat grass and leaves?"

The slightly scared lion cub feeling a sense of frightened joy bleated, "I am a goat. These goats are my family. What else can I eat?"

The Lion roared with dismay and said, "You are a Lion and you eat meat and not grass. Grass is for goats. And don't bleat, you roar." The Lion gave a roar again and the whole forest reverberated with the sound.

The lion cub bleated back and said, "No, I'm a goat. Can't you see?"

The Lion told the cub, "Come with me," and took him to a nearby pond. And then he told the cub, "Look at my face, and now look at the reflection of my face in the still pond."

The lion cub saw the majestic face of the Lion and then saw the reflection of that face in the pond. Then he saw his own reflection in the pond. He became still for a moment which felt like eternity, and then gave out a loud roar, "I am a Lion." The Universe resounded with a joyful cry. I am a Lion.

Awakening the Lion Within

We must discover the origin of our Consciousness. Mere working knowledge and superficial understanding of our existence here in this time and space Universe is a painful one; a goat-like existence for a Lion.

The Story of Crossing the River

How We Miss Out On the Subtleties of Success

All our life we work hard to avoid pain and eke out scraps of pleasure. We read great books and gain knowledge and rarely do we get a real understanding or an experience of who we really are.

I remember my Master telling me repeatedly that mere book knowledge will not do. He used to say to me that mere book knowledge alone is like being a donkey with a load of books.

One day he told me, "When you want to cross a river what do you do? You get a boat and then row the boat to the other bank of the river. Then when you go to the other side, if you don't jump off the boat and step onto the bank you have not crossed the river yet. You might as well have not bothered rowing across the river, fighting the current of the river. Just jump off the boat when you reach the other side. That is why you crossed the river in the first place. Don't stay on the boat."

He continued, "When you want to cross the river then you need a boat and the boat, in this case, is books and knowledge. You need the knowledge to take you to the other side. When you reach the other side then you have to jump off the boat of knowledge and you need to experience the understanding of the other bank of the river. Knowledge is the boat, not the destination. Jumping off the boat is meditation and experiencing the Truth."

Then he used to laugh and say, "Most seekers of truth cross the river but still stay on the boat. They don't jump off the boat; they are really still on the other side of the river. They cling onto the boat."

Just Jump Off the Boat

The Ancient Masters understood the plight of their students in their efforts to jump off the boat. The Masters saw and felt their students' difficulties and frustrations. To make it practical and easy for the students, the Masters formulated the Four Proclamations and the process of meditation; so that the students could jump off the boat and cross the river.

Individuals of all cultures and all educational levels regardless of their social background can practice this meditation and take back control over their own thinking process. They can take back control of their own life. They can think the thoughts they want. They can be a success.

This is the simplest and the easiest way to realize the Truth. The Four Proclamations will flood and purgate all negativity out of the mind. Your mind is like the well and your Consciousness is like the Ocean. What good is a well when there is a flood?

CHAPTER 13

THE SECRET OF ALL SECRETS FOR SUCCESS

The Unfailing System of Success of the Ancients Revealed through the Four Proclamations

The Four Proclamations can release the mind from the shackles of the intellect. These four eternal principles can free the mind from past conditioning, the limitations of the present circumstances, and the fear of the future.

These Proclamations can give you the ability to think out of the box and to realize the Truth; the Truth that will set you free to be what you want to be.

You will be able to think the thoughts that you want to think. In essence, you will no longer be a prisoner of your circumstances. You will become the Master of your world and the designer of your own destiny.

Union is Not Unity

You will experience Unity, the bliss that passeth all understanding. To experience Unity is the goal of the individual while in the physical body. This is the Teaching and the objective of the Ancient Traditions. Unless you experience this Unity, which is different from union, you will not be able to know yourself. The need to recognize the difference between Unity and union is absolutely important to understand and experience the Four Proclamations.

Union is when two or more people or states get united with a belief or a cause or a purpose. In union there is still an element of separation. The united entities continue to be separate but happen to be grouped together. Unity on the other hand, is when you realize that you are one with the Universe. There is no separation anywhere. The Ancients, to emphasize this meaning when speaking about Unity, always ended their expression with "not two." Like in the phrase, "I and the Universe are One, not two."

Moses, in the *Bible*, as a part of the preamble to the *Ten Commandments* said, "God is One." He did not say that there is only one God. He was delivering the Commandments to those who already worshipped One God. The key to understanding the *Ten Commandments* is to know and experience Unity. The Hebrew word for Unity is *Echud* which means One. It means Unity or One, not two. He was not in any way referring to any form of union. He was expressing Unity.

This leads us directly to understanding our relationship with the Universe, or God. Knowing this relationship is vital to our success. And that has been the Teaching of the Ancients throughout time to this day.

When we say, "I and the Universe are One," what do we actually mean by it? When Jesus of Nazareth said, "I and my Father are One," what did he mean by it?

Take a few moments to ponder over it and objectively try to give an answer. Your answer, your objective answer, will make a big difference in your life.

We know that God doesn't end anywhere and that He is Infinite and Eternal. If He ended anywhere, then He could not be God because God is Infinite and Eternal without beginning and ending. Therefore we can safely conclude that God does not end somewhere and I begin from where God ends. This is a ridiculous idea isn't it? It makes God finite because it says that God ends somewhere.

Unity cannot be understood by the intellect and neither can it be explained in words, in any language. When you will experience Unity you will become speechless, you will become silent. You will become ecstatic and euphoric. Ecstasy and euphoria cannot be spoken about or written about. You just become silent.

The mind intellectually rejects any thought of Unity or being One with the Universe and does not allow this Truth to enter your heart. The Ancients understood this and so they devised instruments to train the mind for realizing the Truth, that you and the Universe are One, *God is One*. These instruments are the Four Proclamations; the Secrets of which are about to be revealed to you.

My Master used to tell me that the world is a play of the ocean and the drop of the ocean. The ocean is the Universe and the drop of the ocean is the Individual. The drop of the ocean has all the qualities of the ocean. He used to also say that a spark from the blaze of a fire has all the power of the blaze and can create the same blaze. This is the way the Ancients explained Unity and this can give you glimpses of what is meant by the declaration of Jesus of Nazareth, "I and my Father are One."

The huge icebergs floating in the ocean look so separate from the ocean. They look so different and solid and yet we know for certain that the entire iceberg was made by the ocean and with the ocean and is the ocean. It is the play of the ocean. We also know that the iceberg and the ocean are one. The iceberg's entire quest of life is to merge back into the ocean and become the ocean. That is the path of return of the iceberg.

When the iceberg melts into the ocean it becomes the ocean. When the drop of the ocean enters back into the ocean it loses its identity as a drop and becomes the ocean. Then there is no difference and there is no contradiction between the ocean and the iceberg, between the drop of the ocean and the ocean. Try to visualize the idea that you are the drop of the ocean and Consciousness is the ocean. Can you feel it? Meditate on it.

Experience This Meditation

To experience this feeling of Unity, I often take a glass of water and put a cube of ice in it. Then I see how the solid ice, apparently so different from the glass of water in every way, melts into the water and becomes the water. The hard cold ice transforms into the fluid water. When our hardened mind melts into the Infinite Consciousness we become what we always were.

That is why St. John's Gospel begins with the concept of Unity poetically composed, "All things were made by him and without him was not anything made that was made." (John 1:3) Herein is the understanding of Unity both from the material and Spiritual point of view.

Ancient Traditions

The great Ancient traditions throughout the world both in the East and West elucidate the same teachings.

In Ancient Egypt the Great Hermes revealed the secret of Unity to his disciples. They came to him from the far reaches of the Earth. They sat at his feet, and tasted the nectar of Unity. He declared the Truth, "….As the Macrocosm so the Microcosm and as the Microcosm so the Macrocosm. ….As all things are from One by the mediation of One so all things have their birth from this One thing…."

The Sacred texts of India, the *Vedas* declare, "As the Universe so the Individual and as the Individual so the Universe."

St. Paul says, "For in him we live, and move, and have our being." (Acts 17:28) The *Bible* states, "Be still, and know that I am God." (Psalm 46:10)

This is the Truth and knowing this Truth will set us free. Free to be whatever we want to be, do whatever we want to do, and have whatever we want to have. Intellectual understanding is not enough. It must be believed. It must become our knowing. When it becomes our Being then we will realize the Truth and the Truth shall set us free.

We must experience the Truth to make it a knowing. It requires constant reflection on the Truth that Consciousness is the one Life and the sub-stratum which gives rise to our phenomenal Universe. Your Consciousness is the spark and Universal Consciousness is the blaze and they are one and the same. Constantly reflecting on the meaning of this Truth and silencing the constant chatter of the intellect brings this Truth to our realization. This is referred to as crossing over the Ocean of Consciousness.

The Four Proclamations

The Ancient Masters of the *Vedas* knew that this path of realization, as simple as it may look, is treacherous and fraught with obstacles. They formulated four proclamations and called them *The Four Mahavakyam*. These Four Proclamations are the essence of the *Vedas*. The Masters formulated this system of meditation to help us realize the entire Spiritual Wisdom of the *Vedas*, and make it our own.

Meditation on these Four Proclamations will lead the student in knowing and realizing the Truth. He will know who he is and why he is here and where he will be going from here; beyond this he will also recognize what is this place we call "here." This will set him free and he will live an anxiety free life, a life of constant bliss.

The following section will lead you through the meaning of the Four Proclamations and the Process of Meditation.

CHAPTER 14

HOW TO TAKE CONTROL OF THE MIND WITH THE POWER OF THE FOUR PROCLAMATIONS

We never learn anything; we discover what we already know. The entire Universe is in us now. All the power that ever was or will be is in you right now. You are a center of expression of that power and through your individualized Consciousness it takes form in thought and word. When you are immersed in this understanding you are guided step by step into the path of liberation. To lead you through this journey to know your Self is the purpose of the Four Proclamations.

Thousands of years ago in the forests and the mountains of the Himalayas the Ancient Masters formulated a system. It was a system to train the mind to experience the relationship between the Individual and the Universe, between man and God. This system consists of four statements; rather, they are the Four Proclamations which lead man to his liberation from all bondage.

These Proclamations have parallels in the Ancient teachings of the world. They contain the essence of all the teachings of the *Vedas*, the Sacred texts of India. These Proclamations have been tested and tried for thousands of years by the great sages and Masters leading the neophyte or the student into Self Mastery.

The practice of these principles gives the power to the student to realize and experience that Consciousness is the One life, from which the whole phenomenal Universe emerges. Consciousness is the life force of all matter, sentient and insentient. All the power of this magnificent Universe is in your Consciousness now, at this very moment. By controlling your own mind you can control your world. This practice will give you back your control over your own mind.

All the power is in you, you do not get the power; you realize what you already have. It was always with you but it was under the control of your mind. And now with this practice you will control your own mind. You will think from the core of your Being; your thinking will almost blend into the enchanting world of fantasy. You will be able to vision things that you could not vision before, what you considered impossible will become possible. It won't be fantasy for you; it will be your reality. Then you can "Dream the impossible dream." Then you will realize the meaning of *All things are possible with God.*

Meditation on the Four Proclamations

Four Mahavakyam

Mahavakyam Meditation will be like peeling away layer after layer of an onion. While you are peeling the onion, your eyes will water. When all the layers are peeled away you will find your true Self at the Center, and you will realize the No-Thing out of which the whole Universe has emerged. Then you too can say, "I and the Universe are One," "I Am That I Am," "I am the Cause and the substance."

Externally nothing will look different. You will still do your grocery shopping and you will still do your daily chores and you will still watch TV. Yet you will enter the silence and become silent. There are no words to describe this feeling and this realization. You will not be dependent on conditions, you will be thinking from outside the box.

The human mind is unformed in the beginning and takes on the form of its environment. The thinking process is formed by the conditions present around us. Our environment usually produces thoughts of limitations which lead us to living in denial of our True Power. Limitations are denial of our Divinity. This denial is considered as living a negative existence. Liberation is breaking free from this life of denial and entering your True Unlimited Being. You will realize that you live in Eternity and you are enjoying the sport of existence.

The Path of Return

The path of return to your True Being is the goal of life. It is established by realizing your own ability to achieve any goal that you set without depending on any conditions past, present, and future. It will open up your power to Vision from the Absolute and the Unconditioned. You will experience directly the relationship of your mind with your Consciousness. You will experience Unity. Just like the baby in the mother's womb is One with the mother and is never concerned with sustenance. You will realize that your umbilical cord with Universal Consciousness never was and never can be severed. Then you will know that Consciousness is your total supply and your sustenance.

Mind Is Made Clear By Meditation

Understanding these Four Proclamations and meditating on them will lead you to the Truth and make you free. Meditation on The Four Proclamations gives you back your control over your own mind.

My Master used to tell me, "Never forget three things, first, never forget God or the Universe which is the Cause and the substance of all. Constantly remember God, the Cause of your Being. Second, never forget your enemy. Always keep a constant vigil over your enemy and keep him very close to you. Finally, remember my son, that you have no enemies."

He continued with a little affectionate smile, "The only enemy you have is your own mind. It is your mind that makes you and it is also your mind that breaks you. It can make you into a King and it also can make you into a Pauper. You must have full control over your mind at all times."

The Mind is the Processor and Consciousness is the Operator. When the Processor takes over control of the Operator you have Chaos. Isn't that the case all around us? The residents of the mental institutions all over the world are the living proof of this condition. This condition occurs when the mind has taken full control of an individual's Consciousness. Many of us suffer a mild attack of this once in a while from time to time. You don't have to be a resident of a mental institution to suffer from this ailment.

The Four Proclamations were formulated to give you back your control over your mind; make it your best friend to serve you and make you into a King and not a Pauper. This meditation will give you the realization of your true Self. You will know who you are and you will have command and control over your mind and your life. You will decide what you want to think and manifest the thought with ease.

You will know how to think from the depths of your Consciousness by realizing how the Universe thinks. You will know how to act, freed from the mind's dictates of limitations, by realizing how the Universe Acts. When you speak, you will speak from the core of your Being and your voice will carry the power of the Universe.

To practice this meditation, it is necessary that you clearly understand what these Four Proclamations mean not only intellectually but by entering into the spirit of the Proclamations. The Ancients formulated this meditation system to overcome your mind's control over your Consciousness. The Mind, in subtle ways, will try to protest against these Proclamations because its grip over you, your Consciousness, will be threatened.

Mind, Body, and Consciousness

The goal of the Ancient Teachings and Philosophy is to take control of the Mind. The Mind is the subtle body and the physical body is the visible and outer layer of the subtle body. The state of the Mind affects the body. We know that the mind is part and parcel of the body. We know this by observation.

Fear changes the vibration of the body. The throat becomes parched and the body becomes prone to paralysis. Joy relaxes the body and puts it at ease. The difference between the Body and Mind is that the Mind is at a higher rate of vibration and the Body is at a lower rate of vibration. Our eyes are only capable of seeing the lower rates of vibration. The Mind is not Consciousness; it is the vehicle of Consciousness and an integral part of the body.

Consciousness is behind the Mind and the foundation of the Mind. Consciousness is the reality and the Creator of your world. Mind is the processor. Matter is Mind at a lower rate of vibration. Both Mind and Body are restricted to time and space. Consciousness is not trapped in time and space. Consciousness is free from the past, present, and the future. It is Unity.

Whatever you are conscious of becomes your reality. When you vision and see the reality of your vision, it is already yours. You know that you have it and you feel the joy of having it. It is not yet in time and space but it is in your heart, which is your Consciousness. The Mind will bring it into the dimensions of time and space if you wait as one who understands; this vision is your reality, the physical manifestation is merely the reflection of your Consciousness.

The Ancient Masters throughout history have given these teachings to their disciples in various forms. Jesus of Nazareth told his disciples,

Therefore I say unto you, What things soever ye desire, when ye pray, believe that ye receive them, and ye shall have them.

- Mark 11:24

Only your Ego can negate the vision of your desire and thereby prevent it from being brought into physical manifestation. According to the great Sage Patanjali, Ego is when you identify the instrument of seeing with the Seer. The Mind is the instrument and the Seer is your Consciousness, like the binoculars are the instrument and You are the Seer. Mind is not Consciousness.

Mind is the instrument of your Consciousness. As mentioned earlier, when you are hungry and tired your memory seems to fail you and you can't remember things and names easily. Then after you have eaten and relaxed you get your memory back. This shows that Mind is not Consciousness, it is a part of the body; the subtle body. In neuroscience there is no duality between the mind and the body. They are one.

Consciousness is not dependent on anything external. It is not bound by time and space. It is the cause of everything external. Consciousness creates and creation is always from No-Thing. Consciousness is the substance of all things. This is what the Mind does not want to accept.

The Four Proclamations bring your Mind back home to Consciousness and develop a loving relationship of total trust. The Mind will rely on Consciousness as a baby will rely on the mother for all its sustenance. The Mind will be living in the absolute comfort and love of Consciousness, the source of All Power and its origin. Your mind will know that all the fear and pain that it had suffered from in the past was only when it did not rely on Consciousness. Your Mind will obey you and become the instrument through which you enter the bliss of limitless life. You are the Master of your world. You are Consciousness and Consciousness is the Creator.

CHAPTER 15

THE FOUR PROCLAMATIONS UNVEILED

The Four Proclamations will be unveiled as follows:

1. The English translation of each of the Four Proclamations will be given, one at a time and in sequence. This will be followed by the phonetic transliteration of each Proclamation in its original language, Sanskrit. This is no longer a commonly spoken language. Sanskrit is used mainly for ceremonies, rituals, and meditations.

2. Next, the purpose and the interior meaning of the Proclamation will be given to create a clear understanding before entering into meditation on it.

3. Then the process of using the Proclamation in meditation will be given.

Purpose Reiterated

Success in life is to take control of your thinking process. To think the thoughts you want to think and bring them into physical manifestation.

These Four Proclamations will give you the awareness of your relationship with the Universe and its grand manifestation. You will begin to know who you are and realize your own authority over your life.

In Ancient Times when the student or the neophyte came to the Master he was told the meaning of one Proclamation at a time. Then the Master told him to continuously repeat the Proclamation till the Master felt the student had internalized it. The student became the Proclamation.

Each Proclamation leads to the next in perfect harmony in order for the student to attain the realization that he and the Universe are One, not two. That He is the Master of his world.

A word of caution is needed here. You cannot skip any Proclamation or go to the Fourth one right away and meditate on it. It will not work. Each Proclamation prepares the mind to accept the next.

The Four Proclamations can be repeated in English or any language of your choice as long as you understand the meaning. You have to internalize the words and make these Proclamations a part of your Being. When these Proclamations were formulated, the spoken language of the time was Sanskrit and that is why the original is in Sanskrit. Sanskrit is the root of most of the Indo-European languages. The sources of the Proclamations are given as and when they are introduced.

The First Proclamation

Consciousness Is the Creator

Sanskrit: *Pragyanaam Brahman*

Phonetic: pra-gya-naam brahm-ha
Source: Rg Veda, Aitareya Upanisad 3.3

In the original text in Sanskrit it is *Pragyanaam Brahman,* translated it means Consciousness is the Creator. *Pragyanaam* means Consciousness. It is your Consciousness, my Consciousness, and Universal Consciousness. There is only one Consciousness.

Brahman means the Creator of the physical Manifested Universe. The word Brahman ends with a slight nasal intonation and the "n" is almost silent. The Universe is Brahman and the Universe is therefore Consciousness. Consciousness is the creative force and also, at the same time, the substance with which the Creation is manifested in its physical form.

The Universe is not limited by substance; it cannot be dependent on anything. It is. It produces substance out of itself. Creation is out of No-Thing. All things are made with Consciousness and by Consciousness.

We know that God or the Universe is Infinite and Unlimited. If God or the Universe were dependent on any substance to work with, then God could not be God, as God cannot be dependent on anything or be limited by anything. That would imply that God ended somewhere and where God ended would be the place where substance began. If that were the case, and we know that it is not, then no one could logically agree that God is Eternal and Infinite, without beginning and ending. God cannot be God unless and until He is Infinite and One and Eternal.

The Universe is substance and substance is Consciousness. It is whole. We know that all substance has Consciousness and is made of Consciousness. An atom has Consciousness as much as a planet has Consciousness. The mineral, the plant, the animal, and man; all are Consciousness.

This Proclamation, *Pragyanaam Brahman – Consciousness Is the Creator*, awakens in you the understanding of the reality of Consciousness. It develops in you the awareness of your relationship with the Universe.

The Sanskrit root *bra* means to bulge or to expand. The word *Brahman* denotes the Universe. The Sanskrit word for the Universe is *Brahmand.* The Universe is continuously expanding. The center of a circle is not separate from the circumference; it is only the expansion of the center into the circumference, the bulging forth of the center.

The center has no dimension. It is In-Visible. As was illustrated in Chapter 10, *Centering Yourself for Success*, you may put a dot at the center to indicate the center; but that dot will become another concentric circle with the same center; it won't be a center. If you put a microscope over the dot you will only see another circle. The circumference is the bulging or the expansion of the dimensionless center. This is the great paradox of existence. Brahman is the center, and the expansion of the center is the circumference which we usually call the circle. The circle is the expansion of the center. Consciousness is the center *and* the circumference; Consciousness is the thought *and* the thing.

The First Proclamation is *Consciousness is the Creator* and in Sanskrit, *Pragyanaam Brahman.*

The Second Proclamation

That Thou Art

Sanskrit: *Tat Tavm Asi*

Phonetic: tat tavam asee
Source: Samaveda, Chandogya Upanisad 6.8.7

In the original text in Sanskrit it is *Tat Tavm Asi. Tat* means That, *Tavm* means Thou and *Asi* means Are or Art.

The Second Proclamation brings you to the realization that everything is Consciousness. Everything that you see, touch, hear, taste, and smell is Consciousness.

This Universe is made with one thing and that thing is the One, Conscious, Intelligent, All Powerful, Energy. The realization of this is the Secret of Success.

Knowing this intellectually is not enough. It needs to become a part of your thinking and feeling. It should become a state of mind. The Creator and the Created are One and the same.

Consciousness is the stuff of all things visible and In-Visible. This idea must saturate your whole Being. This will make you realize your relationship with the Universe.

All things are from the One and all manifestation is made with this thing alone. This One thing is the *Shakti* of the *Vedas*, the *Water of Life* of the *Bible*, and the *One Energy* of the Scientists.

When you meditate on this Proclamation *That Thou Art*, you will feel your Unity. Then you will know that nothing ever happens by accident. There are no accidents. You will see through all appearances.

The Third Proclamation

My Consciousness Is the Creator
Sanskrit: *Ayam Atman Brahman*

Phonetic: ah-yam at-ma brahm-ha
Source: Atharvaveda, Mandukya Upanisad 1.2

In the original text in Sanskrit it is *Ayam Atman Brahman. Ayam* is My, *Atman* is Consciousness, and *Brahman* is the Creator.

This Proclamation confirms the Aphorism, "As the Universe so the Individual and as the Individual so the Universe; As the Macrocosm so the Microcosm and as the Microcosm so the Macrocosm." You, the individual are the spark of the blaze and the Universe or God, the blaze. The power of the blaze and the spark are identical. This cannot be intellectually perceived and thus meditation on this Proclamation will seep its meaning into your Consciousness and become your Being.

This is what the *Bible* refers to as Man being made in the image and likeness of God. This means, that you create your world the same way as God creates.

This Proclamation, *My Consciousness is the Creator*, develops in your Consciousness your indivisibility with the Universe and at the same time gives you your own Identity. You will know that you live and move and have your Being in the Universe and you will also know that you are your own Universe. You will know that your individuality is a center of expression of All Power. It is through you the Universe continues its creation by becoming you.

The Fourth Proclamation

I Am the Creator

Sanskrit: *Aham Brahmasmi*

Phonetic: ah-ham brahm-ash-mee
Source: Yajurveda, Brhadâranyaka Upanisad, 1.4.10

In the original Sanskrit text it is, *Aham Brahmasmi*. *Aham* means I, and *Brahmasmi* means Am the Creator. In essence it is the ultimate declaration of your Identity.

The Ancients knew that this Proclamation would not be accepted by the mind without protest. It is too large a claim for the mind. That is why they formulated the first three Proclamations. These three Proclamations prepare the mind of the student to accept the final Proclamation.

The First Proclamation states that *Consciousness is the Creator*; it prepares the mind to know who and what the Creator is. The Second Proclamation, *That Thou Art*, makes the student realize that everything is the Creator and the substance of everything is also the Creator. There is no difference between the wave and the ocean. The wave is the ocean and inseparable from the ocean.

The Third Proclamation, *My Consciousness Is the Creator*, plants the seed in the mind of the student of the power and function of his Individual Consciousness. However, there still lingers a sense of separation between the Universe and his Individuality. Expressing it as *My Consciousness* shows a sense of possession; anything you posses is not you, it is yours. There is a sense of separation between Consciousness and the owner of Consciousness.

The Fourth Proclamation, *I Am the Creator*, demolishes this sense of separation and reveals to the student his own identity. Now, he knows who he is. You don't become who you are, you realize who you are. You don't become the Creator, you are the Creator. You are Consciousness. I am Consciousness. There is no difference between you and your Consciousness. *Consciousness is the Creator* and everything is Consciousness.

In the *Bible* the Name of God given to Moses is, *I Am That I Am*; The *Vedas* say, *I Am the Creator.*

The heart of this Proclamation, *I Am the Creator*, is the Truth, and there is only one Truth, the Universe is One, not two. You and the Universe are One.

Meditating on this Proclamation will transport you into bliss and joy. Anxiety and Fear will flee before you and you will begin to live in a world of Certainty.

Then you will know the Truth as revealed in the Book of Job, "Thou shalt also decree a thing, and it shall be established unto thee: and the light shall shine upon thy ways." (Job 22:28)

Living in this state of Consciousness, Consciousness of *I Am That I Am,* is the goal of life.

The Ultimate Meditation

The Fourth Proclamation is the culmination of the other three Proclamations for the realization of Unity. The First Proclamation declares, *Consciousness is the Creator*. The Second Proclamation declares, *Everything is Consciousness*. The Third Proclamation declares, *My Consciousness is the Creator*. The Fourth Proclamation, *I Am the Creator*, is the final awareness for realizing your Identity.

The first three Proclamations are the process which leads the mind into the realization, *I Am the Creator*, without resistance. It is a process that coaches the mind to realize the Truth of its existence. There is no separation between the created and the Creator. Consciousness is the substance and the Creator of the substance. *I Am the Creator* translates into *I Am That,* or *That I Am*. This is *The Word*, *I Am That,* and in the *Vedas* it is *So Hum* or *Hamsa*. It is Life and the substance of Life.

The Ancients realized that this understanding, *That I Am* or *I Am the Creator* will not be acceptable to the intellect. The mind would be opposed to even consider meditating upon it, let alone embracing it and experiencing this sublime wisdom. The Masters knew that they had to lead the intellect through the preceding three Proclamations to prepare the mind to enter into this meditation.

Consciousness is the Creator is the first realization, the second realization is *Everything is Consciousness* and the third realization is *My Individualized Consciousness is the Creator*. Up to this stage of realization there is still a sense of separation between the Creator and my Consciousness. Whenever I say "my" or "mine" there is a feeling of possession and possession is separate from the possessor. The Fourth Proclamation declares, *I Am the Creator*. There is no difference between the Creator and the Created. From this Proclamation flows *The Word, That I Am,* the original Sound, *So Hum*. The Life Breath of everything.

When we breathe in, that is when we inhale, we make the sound "So" and when we breathe out or exhale we make the sound "Hum." *So Hum* reversed in Sanskrit is *Hamsa*. Hamsa means *I Am That*. *So Hum* means *That I Am*. Every breath we take is repeating the Fourth Proclamation *That I Am*. Our life began with this Proclamation and when this Proclamation leaves our body, we leave the body.

In the *Vedas, Brahm*a is called *Shabda Brahma*. *Shabda* means sound and it signifies that Sound creates and maintains creation. The New Testament of the *Bible*, St. John's Gospel says, *The Word* is God, and everything is made by *The Word* and with *The Word*. Ancient Traditions throughout the world also allocate creation to Sound and Sound is the Creator. Science confirms what the Ancients declared, that everything physical is Sound.

The sound *So Hum* is repeated involuntarily by an average healthy person about 21,600 times in a day, sleeping or awake. It is our life. The Ancient Greeks called it *Pneuma*. In English, the word spirit comes from Latin, *Spiritus*, which means *I breathe*. In Hebrew, Consciousness is called *Rhuach*, which means *Life Breath*.

The Hindus, in the *Vedas*, call Consciousness *Prana*, which means *Life Breath.* In the *Bible*, God made Adam into a living Soul by breathing life into him through his nostrils. It is agreed by all that *Life Breath* is the Creator and we are Individualized *That.*

Meditation on *The Word*

Meditation on *The Word, So Hum* will release you from your reliance on the mind and on conditions. You will realize the Truth of the Fourth Proclamation, *I Am the Creator* or in Sanskrit, *Aham Brahmasmi.* You will live with assured expectation of everything you desire. You will not be dependent on any condition for the manifestation of your desire. You are the Creator of your World.

During the regular meditation period sit still for at least ten minutes and observe your in breathing and out breathing. Do not try to control your breath. Let it breathe for you. Every breath is saying to you, *That I Am* or *I Am That.* This is a natural meditation that you were endowed with in your mother's womb. You will continue to meditate on it, whether you are aware of it or not, till you pass on. Then *The Word* will leave your body and without *The Word* the body will not be able to hold itself together with all its parts. It will decompose.

Every single creature, every tree and plant, every single planet and galaxy, every grain of sand, and everything in the Universe is made of *The Word,* with *The Word,* and is repeating *The Word. The Word* is *That I Am* or the Fourth Proclamation *Aham Brahmasmi, I Am the Creator.*

You are the spark of the blaze and the spark has all the power of the blaze to create the same blaze. You are the drop of the Ocean and all the Ocean is in the drop of the Ocean. The Masters have known this and have told you, "As the Macrocosm so the Microcosm and as the Microcosm so the Macrocosm." The *Vedas* declare, "As the Universe so the Individual, as the Individual so the Universe." In Sanskrit it is pronounced, *Yat Brahmand Tat Pind, Yat Pind Tat Brahmand.* The *Bible* states, "I and my Father are One," (John 10:30) and "All things that the Father hath are mine." (John 16:15) Then the *Bible* states, "Be still, and know that I Am God." (Psalm 46:10)

When you merge your mind with your Consciousness, *That I Am*, you have become the Master of your Thought and you have taken control of your world. You can think the thoughts you want to think and you will manifest every single desire which you have thought from the Absolute and the Unconditioned. You have become a success. You will be in bliss. You will become still. You will become silent. You will not be able to say and express how you feel. And you will still continue to change diapers and go grocery shopping.

There is an old Sufi story which will express to you how you will feel when you reach this stage.

CHAPTER 16

THE STORY OF THE WALLED CITY

How a Successful Man Relates to His Environment

There was a city surrounded by a wall so big that nobody could see what was outside the city. The citizens of the city could only see the sky and what was in the city.

Everyone that scaled up the straight wall and stood on top of the wall, jumped off the wall. They never came back. So no one in the city knew what was on the other side of the wall. This got everybody curious and they wanted to find out what was there outside.

The Mayor of the City called a council meeting to find out ways and means to know what was outside the city. In the Council meeting a young man came up with a brilliant idea. He said, "If we select one of us to climb up the wall and before that person climbs the wall we should tie a rope to his feet, and when he jumps we will pull him back. This way we can find out what is there, outside the city."

Everybody clapped and gave him a standing ovation. The Council, owing to the young man's brilliance, selected him to do the job. They had their ceremony for this big occasion and they were waiting with controlled patience for all these rituals to be over with to find out what is out there.

The man scaled the wall. The whole population of the city watched with bated breath to know the truth. The man stood on top of the wall. The people below saw the man's face gleam with ecstasy. Like everyone before him, he too helplessly jumped. The city folks let out a grand cheer. He was pulled back and brought to the city square.

They asked, "Tell us, Oh our Hero what did you see?"

The people waited for the Truth. The young man became silent. He could not say anything.

When you will know the Truth, you too will become silent. There are no words in any language to express what you will experience, when you have scaled the wall of your mind through meditation, and see what lies beyond. Anything you say will only sound like gibberish to those who don't know. Silence will prevail in your life and you will live in bliss.

CHAPTER 17

MEDITATION AND VISUALIZATION IN THE SUCCESS PROCESS

What the Ancient Masters Taught Their Students

Before you begin to meditate on the Proclamations you must know the difference between Visualization and Meditation. Meditation clears the mind and makes you realize your Unity; it liberates your mind from dependency on the external, the world of effects. It makes you free to Vision your heart's desire and not just what you need to get through the day, or to get through your life.

Meditation shows you that you are Consciousness and that Consciousness is perfect intelligence, not a blind mechanical energy. The energy of Consciousness made you and is you. To Vision on the other hand refers to the fact that all things made by this energy are made by what the Ancients called *adaptation* or Visualization.

Meditation gives you the power to create visions and manifest the visions from the Unconditioned and the Absolute. You cannot be without a vision for a single moment of your life, but the visions that you carry and manifest are not always what you want. They may be fear visions, which we call worry, and even though you don't want to carry such visions, you still do carry them helplessly. Meditation clears the mind and gives you your power over your mind to vision what you want to vision.

The substance of all things is the One energy. Meditation brings this realization to the surface of your Consciousness. You realize that there is no other force or energy that can negate or neutralize this One energy.

Your mind is the instrument through which you create intention. Intention triggers Imagination. Visualization organizes Imagination into a Vision. The purpose of meditation is to take back control of your mind; then you will have the freedom to visualize what you want and manifest it.

Chapter 20 will present the **Four Steps to Visioning and Manifesting the Vision** and you will be guided through the process and the spirit of Visualization.

The meditations you are about to enter here are for the purpose of taking back control of your mind. You can think the thoughts that you want to think. You can think out of the box and set visions from the Absolute and the Unconditioned. You will experience your Oneness with the Universe. You will be the Master of your destiny.

You will live in bliss even while you are engaged in navigating through the world of multitasking and doing business at the speed of thought. Unclear mind produces unclear vision. Meditation clears the mind.

Unclear mind Produces Unclear Vision

When you meditate on a statement you enter into the spirit of the statement. You become absorbed in the meaning of it. You become the statement. It becomes your Being. Words and outer meanings of the statement fall off like ripened fruit falling off a tree; you and the statement become One. You silence the internal chatter of your mind. You free your Consciousness from limiting memories. The feeling, of the statement or the thought or the words, gains unrestricted entry into your heart and forms your Being; it penetrates through your Consciousness and goes deep into your sub-consciousness.

Every word, every statement, and every object has two aspects; the outer and the inner, the subtle and the gross, or the center and the circumference. They are One and the same.

In meditation you separate the subtle from the gross and enter the essence or the center of the statement. When you churn milk the butter which is hidden in the milk, and is the essence or inner aspect of the milk, floats to the top. The milk separates into whey and butter and you cannot mix them back together again. The ice in a glass of water will melt into the water. The ice becomes the water and you cannot separate the water of the ice from the water that was in the glass. The ice is your conditioned mind which surrenders to Consciousness, the water which it is, and becomes One with

Consciousness. The butter is the essence of your Being which surfaces through meditation so you know who you are.

You too will realize the essence of your Being. You too will know that you are pure Consciousness and everything that you intend is already yours. You will know that you are the embodiment of Consciousness. You are everywhere and everywhen. Your personal Identity is like a whirlpool in the Ocean of Consciousness.

Meditation on the Proclamations will be like churning milk and the essence of the Truth, the butter of the Proclamation, will become your knowing and cease to be just a belief. Then you will live and move and have your Being in that feeling and knowing. "All obscurity will flee before you," and you will realize your own glory, the glory of the Universe. Remember that the butter churned out can never again mix back with the milk.

As I mentioned earlier, we don't learn anything; we only discover what we already know. Your Consciousness knows itself; your mind does not. At most it may have a very faint idea. The mind wants you to believe that it is all there is. It wants you to believe that there is nothing greater than itself.

Repeating these Proclamations one at a time as you will be shown will be like wiping off layers of dust covering your mind. Your mind is like a pair of eyeglasses through which you look out into the world and through which you look at yourself. Meditating on these Proclamations will clear the glasses and you will see the world as it truly is and you will see yourself as you truly are.

You are bliss and joy. You and the Universe are One. You too will know the true meaning of the words of The Ancients and these words will resonate in your heart as they resonated in the hearts of the Ancients, "As the Universe so the Individual, as the Individual so the Universe; As the Macrocosm so the Microcosm and as the Microcosm so the Macrocosm."

Then we will see who we are and discover our relationship with the Universe and banish anxiety and doubt, the cause of all negativity, from our life. This is what is meant when we say meditation clears the mind.

Then we will know the meaning of St. Paul's statement, "For now we see through a glass, darkly; but then face to face: now I know in part; but then shall I know even as also I am known."
(1 Corinthians 13:12)

Four Components of Meditation

The first component is posture of body. In Sanskrit this is called ***Asana***. The word *Asana* means seat; to sit. Posture starts with the body. When the body is in a comfortable position it allows the mind and the intellect to concentrate and focus at the center. In all our actions in life we start with posture, or how we position ourselves. Our posture determines our attitude.

The second component is to hold the mind on a particular word, statement or object. In Sanskrit this is called ***Dharana***. The word *Dharana* simply means to hold with the purpose of accepting and internalizing.

The third component is continuous concentration, which means the unbroken flow of attention on the object, word, or statement. In Sanskrit this is called ***Dhyana.*** It means concentration with prolonged attention. Concentration is being at the center of the object of meditation.

The fourth component is to become one with the object of meditation by holding the mind on it and by continuous concentration on the object of meditation. You become one with the object, the word or the statement. All forms and the external fall off and you become the essence of the statement, word or object. In Sanskrit this is called ***Samadhi.*** It means becoming the same. When the ice melts into the water there is *Samadhi.* The ice becomes the water.

CHAPTER 18

THE ART
OF
MEDITATION

Silencing the Internal Chatter of the Mind

In this section you will be given the application of the components of meditation and the four steps of the process of meditating on the Proclamations. Even if you have never meditated before just follow these steps and you will find the process to be simple and easy.

The First Step for Meditation
Posture

The first step in any meditation is posture. That is how you position yourself, physically, emotionally, and spiritually. Sit in a comfortable position, where you will have minimum awareness of your body. The Lotus position, for those of you who know it, is as good as sitting on a straight back chair.

If you are sitting on a chair, sit straight and place your feet flat on the floor. Rest your hands on your lap in a relaxed position. Hold your head upright and straight on your shoulders. You must feel comfortable. Do not strain yourself in any way. If you feel any kind of strain, make an adjustment to feel comfortable.

The object of the exercise is to be comfortable and allow a free flow of energy through your body. This is *Asana*, the first component of meditation.

Closing your eyelids, turn your eyes slightly upwards and concentrate between your eyebrows. This point between your eyebrows should be your point of focus and concentration on the physical level.

Take four deep breaths. Breathe in through your nostrils and take notice of when the incoming breath stops for a moment, before the out breathing begins. Breathe out through your nostrils. Take notice of the pause that occurs when the out breathing ends and the in breathing begins, and then again when the in breathing ends and the out breathing begins. Do not hold the breath artificially, at all. It must be natural. The pauses will increase, the more you practice this meditation.

Continue to breathe through your nostrils. Do not breathe in or out through your mouth during the meditation. Keep your mouth closed in a relaxed way throughout.

You must allocate a certain amount of time for each period of meditation, ten minutes or fifteen minutes or even five minutes.

These periods will increase as your practice continues and your comfort level and the urge to experience the bliss increases.

Discipline is necessary for success. In the beginning set a time no less than five minutes in the morning after you get ready to start the day. Allow the same period in the evening before you retire for the night. At midday set aside another time slot to meditate if you can find a quiet place.

Now you are ready to start the meditation on the Proclamations. To review, the Four Proclamations are:

The First Proclamation:	**Consciousness Is the Creator** *Pragyanaam Brahman*
The Second Proclamation:	**That Thou Art** *Tat Tavm Asi*
The Third Proclamation:	**My Consciousness Is the Creator** *Ayam Atman Brahman*
The Fourth Proclamation:	**I Am the Creator** *Aham Brahmasmi*

Meditate on one Proclamation at a time in its order from the First to the Fourth. Allocate one week for each of the Proclamations. Don't rush and go to the Fourth before you have meditated on the other three. You will feel the changes even after the first day of your meditation on the First Proclamation.

Even outside the time you've allocated for meditation, carry the awareness of the Proclamation that you are meditating upon. You will want to feel the joy of this awareness.

When you have completed the first four weeks of meditation, then continue to meditate daily on the Fourth Proclamation. Before you start your daily meditation on the Fourth Proclamation, briefly meditate upon the other three by repeating them a few times. I suggest at least four times for each Proclamation. Then when you meditate on the Fourth Proclamation, all the other three Proclamations will come into play in your mind.

The Second Step for Meditation
Holding the Proclamation in Your Mind

The second step for Meditation is holding the Proclamation in your mind by repeating it rhythmically, either silently or audibly for the length of time you have selected to meditate. I find audible repetition more effective than silent repetition.

Audible repetition resonates like a tuning fork and makes your body, mind, and intellect, your physical instruments, be saturated with the sound of the Proclamations. It may be important to mention here that in the Ultimate Meditation on *The Word* there is no repetition, there is only observation of the *The Word*, your life breath.

Give a pause of at least one second between the repetitions of each Proclamation. You can meditate using the Sanskrit form of the Proclamation or the English, whichever you feel comfortable with, as both are equally effective.

During the day, outside your allocated time for meditation, whenever you get a chance, repeat the Proclamations; silently if you are among other people and audibly when you are alone. This will make your mind hold on to the Proclamation; this is *Dharana,* the second component for meditation.

In this step you focus your mind onto one single idea, to the exclusion of any other. It is like pointing your mind in one direction like a beam of light which you can cast on any object. You go inward, deep into your Consciousness, and feel the reality of your Being. You can achieve this through ongoing meditation. Your mind will be made to hold on to this idea even amidst your daily work.

The Third Step for Meditation
Continuous Concentration on the Proclamation

The third step flows in from the second step seamlessly. When the mind is focused, it spontaneously flows into contemplation and reflection on the Proclamation. You enter the heart of the meaning of the Proclamation which the intellect cannot reach. The mind feels; the intellect decides. The holding of the Proclamation in focus and contemplating on it, silences the intellect and your mind will feel the joy and bliss of the Truth of the Proclamation. You enter into the knowledge of the Proclamation; this is *Dhyana*, the third component for meditation.

The Fourth Step for Meditation
Becoming One with the Proclamation

The fourth step is prolonged meditation on the Proclamation. You saturate your Being with the feeling of your meditation; you become the Proclamation. You soak your mind with the feeling and become one with it. All outer meanings fall off and you enter into the stillness; you become One with the Proclamation. You know, and no words can express your feeling, you become silent. You just know.

You carry this realization sub-consciously even when you come out of the meditation and do your daily work. You don't even realize consciously why you feel so calm and confident. During the prolonged meditation you realize and become The Proclamation; this is *Samadhi*, the fourth component for meditation.

You can enter into *Samadhi*, not only while you are meditating in your allocated time, but even in the midst of your busy day. Prolonged meditation becomes effortless as you carry these Proclamations with you all the time while working, shopping or playing with your children.

The spirit of the Proclamations saturates your Body, Mind and Spirit. You free your mind from all limitations that hold you. You create your own Vision from the Absolute and take command over your mind. You think the thoughts that you want to think and not the thoughts that you are made to think by your circumstances. You live in a world of thoughts and you have command over your world because you rule your thoughts. You are a Success.

CHAPTER 19

HOW TO VISION AND MANIFEST THE VISION

Before entering into the Four Steps to Visioning and Manifesting the Vision it is important to ask and know "Who is visioning?" and "What is the Substance with which the Vision is brought into Manifestation?" The answer is Consciousness, your *I Am*, is visioning, and is also the Substance with which the Vision is manifested.

Science confirms that matter is energy and energy is Consciousness. The Ancients knew this and they gave this energy various names; in India they called it *Shakti*, in China they named it *Chi* and in the *Bible* it is called the *Water of Life*. All these names refer to Consciousness which is *I Am*. It is the Substance and Power that brings all visions into material manifestation.

I Am are the two most powerful words that impact our lives. These two words determine our state of mind which in turn determines our circumstances. Our circumstances do not make our lives. They only show us our present state of mind, our *I Am*. The Ancient teachings emphasize this again and again because this Truth is the foundation for success. You can be whatever you want to be if you just know the impact of these two words in your life. Your *I Am* defines you. It is you.

The Truth about our *I Am-ness* and its effect in our lives cannot be overemphasized. We see it on Mount Sinai when Moses asks God what His name is. God declares his Name to Moses,

> *And God said unto Moses, I Am That I Am: and he said, Thus shalt thou say unto the children of Israel, I Am hath sent me unto you.*
> - Exodus 3:14

In the *Bhagavad-Gita* the Lord tells Arjuna, "I Am your Consciousness .... Omnipresent: Eternal without beginning and ending."

Both these Ancient texts confirm that Consciousness is the Creator and your Consciousness which is your *I* is the same as Universal Consciousness.

At this juncture it is important to understand the meaning of the word *Man* and the word Mind as they are the navigating instruments that we use to build visions and manifest them.

The word *Man* comes from the Sanskrit root *MN* which is a unit of weight, about forty kilograms. In Ancient times it was used for measuring and distributing the harvest. Man is the Distributor or the Measurer of the Substance of the Universe, which is Infinite without beginning and ending.

The word *Mind* is derived from the root *MN,* as is the word *Man,* and Man is Mind. Man is the distributor of Universal Consciousness. The mind distributes by visioning what it wants to be, do and have. Visioning is measuring out and distributing Infinite Consciousness. When you are Visioning, you are creating a mold and measuring and distributing Infinite Consciousness. The Ancients called it finitizing the Infinite. The Infinite still remains Infinite.

Your Consciousness is not your mind. The mind is the measuring mechanism with which you name and limit Consciousness, the Universal Substance. Your *I* is Consciousness and your *Am* is your mindset or state of mind. Whatever we add to *I Am* defines our Beingness, how we see ourselves. When we say, *I am hungry* or *I am happy* or *I am ecstatic* or *I am rich* we are indicating our Beingness: hungry, happy, ecstatic, rich.

How you define your *I Am* determines what you are and what you think. That becomes your mindset. And your mindset makes your world. You have the freedom to change your mindset and change your world by realizing that your Consciousness is the same as Universal Consciousness. This is accomplished by constant contemplation and meditation on the Four Proclamations. The Final Proclamation proclaims *I Am the Creator* and *That I Am.*

Anything that you hold in your mind and believe that you will have, will manifest as your circumstances. Worrying is visioning. When you worry, you hold a vision of what you fear will happen in your life. Fear is a belief. It is your Consciousness and your mindset, and it will manifest if you do not change your Vision. When you know the power of your *I Am* you can change it in an instant and if you do so, your worry will not manifest. There is a saying that whatever you fear will come upon you. It has to. It is science; *As you sow so shall you reap*. This is how everything is created, from the chair you may be sitting on now, to the entire Universe.

We live in a thought world and our thoughts produce our world. The meditation on the Four Proclamations gives your mind the freedom to think the thoughts you want to think and live in a world of your choosing.

Your Individual Consciousness is the same as Universal Consciousness. When you know this, your whole Being is saturated with this feeling. Only then will you be able to Vision with an Unlimited mind, and physically manifest your Vision with certainty. You will know your Power and you will ask the Power, and the Power will give unfailingly; this is the secret behind the command, "Ask and Receive."

Now we will embark on the most enchanting journey of life, to Vision and Manifest the Vision with certainty.

CHAPTER 20

FOUR STEPS TO VISIONING

How to Vision and Get What You Want

Life is a series of one Vision following another. Every moment of our life we hold a Vision in our mind. The Vision that we hold makes our happiness or our sadness; it creates our moods and our well being. We vision spontaneously throughout the day and even in our sleep when we dream. We don't usually decide to vision and then start visioning. Every waking moment we automatically hold a Vision or see a picture and live out that picture. We must take control and consciously vision what we want.

The question is do we control our Visions or do the Visions which we hold control our life? Can we Vision what we want to Vision? Each Vision that we hold makes us what we are. If we consciously choose the Vision of what we want to be, do, and have, then we take control of our life and our destiny.

Not a single action is made without a Vision. Those who do not make a conscious effort to form and project their own Visions, manifest somebody else's visions. They are floating on a river of borrowed visions and are being buffeted around and through all the turbulences and whirlpools of life without knowing what they want out of life. They have unconsciously agreed to live out their life in concealed hopelessness. They have concealed this hopelessness so deeply that they are unaware that they live in camouflaged hopelessness. They don't know where they will be and where they are going to. They let their environment picture their life for them. They need a Vision and if they don't have a Vision of their own, they will continue to live out the visions of others.

Everything that we do is at first a Vision and then it is an action. All action needs a Vision. When I say I am going to brush my teeth, I see a picture of brushing the teeth with all its details and in full color and sound. I may not be aware of all the details, but I know I saw with my mind's eye, all the details that I will go through when I finish brushing my teeth. It is so automatic that I don't notice it. If you are conscious about it, before you physically brush your teeth, you will see the entire picture of you brushing the teeth like you would see a movie.

A Vision starts with Intention; it is the first step of Visioning. From Intention flow the remaining three steps to Visioning and Manifesting the Vision. The second step is Imagination. The third step is Vision the Mental Picture, and the fourth step is Manifestation.

Step One: Intention

Everything starts with Intention. Intention to manifest an Idea is the first act of Visioning and Manifesting the Vision; where you decide consciously what you want in your life. You take control of your thoughts.

The first step is to enter into the world of ideas. According to the Ancient Greek Master, Plato, this is the Archetypal world, the world of Intention. The Archetype is the original model in your mind, the 'Will' to be something or be someone. Suppose you think of the idea of being rich; your Will to be rich is the idea. The word *idea* means, *I see*.

What you see when you "Will" to be rich could be golfing all day, sailing, living in a condo on the beach, cruising around the world and writing romantic novels, or hundreds of other ideas. You will see all the forms of rich lifestyles. This is the seed of the Vision. In the seed is the tree and all the fruits. The mighty banyan tree sleeps in the seed which is smaller than a grain of sand. Your Intention is the seed.

As we have seen in the chapter on *Centering Yourself for Success*, the Center of a Circle is the Intention and it is also the substance of the Circle. Similarly, everything in the Universe has a center from which it is manifested. The character and form of everything and every situation depends on your Intention, the Archetype, which is the seed of what you want.

All creation starts with Intention. Your life is the sum total of your Intentions. You cannot live without an Intention. Even having no Intention is an Intention to not have an Intention.

The more control you have over your mind to think the thoughts that you want to think, the more control you will have over your Intention and over your life. Your power to intend what you really want depends on your recognition and realization that Consciousness Creates.

Intention is the motive power. In art it is called the motif. The artist begins with a motif and the motif releases the power of Imagination of the artist. Imagination brings forth the play of the brush and the paint on the canvas with Consciousness of the artist to create the Intended masterpiece.

When you intend to be rich the motif is comfort, luxury, and a worry-free life. When you intend to travel around the world your motif may be bliss, discovery, joy and the thrill of seeing exotic places and meeting exciting people. You get a feeling, a sensation, and you feel the passion of the Intention. This is your Being, which is your *I Am*. You feel you already have it.

Many people have told me that they cannot feel this way about Intention; they cannot concentrate on their Intention. I have on occasion presented the following idea. When you worry, you are displaying that you have the power to intend and concentrate. You cannot take your mind off the picture of your worry. Your worry becomes your reality. You cannot eat, sleep or even think. You feel numb and scared. You become irritable and if the worry is of a serious nature it shows up as a health problem. You know how to intend and you do have the power to concentrate; the only difference is that your mind is now more prone to fear than it is to joy.

Fear attracts the slings and arrows of life. Fear is an Intention to have something or some situation even though you don't want to have it. Courage, on the other hand, turns the slings and arrows away. Courage is also an Intention but it is an Intention of living from strength and from the heart, and not from the mind. Meditate on the Four Proclamations and free your mind.

The Secret to Success is to know your power and to know that Consciousness is the only power that creates. You are One with that power. When you have an Intention you have to let go and know that this All Power will bring all the circumstances, conditions, and people to manifest your Intention. You don't do anything; you just see it being done.

Consciousness synchronizes everything and brings the people, the circumstances, and all the ways and means to manifest your Intention. Your Consciousness will organize the Manifestation of your Intention impeccably if you don't interfere with its work.

Being concerned about results and being anxious about the outcome and worrying about the future is interfering with the work of your Consciousness. It is your mind's desire to fail.

Knowing that whatever you intend will be done is the secret of success. This knowing can only come by recognizing and realizing that Consciousness is the only Creative Power in the Universe and there is no other power that can negate it.

This is what the *Bhagavad-Gita* calls non attachment and states clearly to act but do not be concerned how your Intention will manifest. Just know that you don't do anything, you see it being done already, and it is done. You must know what you want and be very specific about your Intention. Jesus of Nazareth taught this to his disciples, "Take therefore no thought for the morrow," which means carry no anxious thoughts.

Concentrated Intention ignites a burning desire within you. Desire and Intention become an irresistible force that form a Vision.

When Intention is planted in Consciousness you will feel that you already have what you intended to have. You will feel the reality of your Intention. Then your concentration on your Intention will transport you into the second step of Visioning and Manifesting the Vision; it is the Creative World, the world of Imagination fuelled by Desire.

The most important action you can take now is to write out your Intention. Do not leave it for a later or a better time. You may change it if your Intention changes. Do not try to remember. Writing crystallizes thought. Start a journal and begin by writing first what you want to Be, Do and Have. Be Specific.

Step Two: Imagination

We live in a world we have imagined. We have created the world that we inhabit with the only creative power, our Imagination. Imagination is the substance of the Creative World. It is the eye of your Consciousness. Your Intention is the purpose. Your Imagination then creates the Vision of what you will be having and doing, when you will accomplish your purpose. Intention is the Beingness and Imagination is the having and doing.

Intention is the seed which is your Beingness. The best analogy I can think of is that if you want to harvest apples you need to plant apple seeds. You cannot plant a mango seed and imagine having a harvest of apples. Beingness is the planting and having is the harvesting. You have to be rich to get riches. *Consciousness is the Creator* and your Beingness creates.

Life is thinking and feeling. It is your Consciousness, it is your state of mind. What you think and feel throughout the day is your Beingness. When you think and feel rich you will become rich. Your Consciousness creates.

We live in a world we have imagined and created. We can change our world by changing our Imagination. Imagination forms patterns or molds and fills the molds with substance that it produces out of itself. Imagination is not subject to any conditions of substance or situations. Imagination creates its own conditions and substance to fill the molds and the matrices that it forms to bring the Intention to Manifestation.

Imagination is pictures in motion and these pictures are generated by feeling and your feeling is generated from your desire. Desire is not a fancy or a fantasy, it is real. It is more real than the things that you see around you.

True desire is when your whole Being is soaked in the image of your desire and you cannot see the difference between your desire and the physical world around you. Desire is the dynamo that produces the Imagination which brings the desire into physical Manifestation.

To free your Imagination from the clutches of your mind you must constantly dwell on your desire and continuously purify your desire. What does that mean? It means that if you cannot dwell on your desire all the time, you don't believe your desire will manifest in the physical world. To purify your desire is to constantly be vigilant that you don't depend on any conditions whatsoever for the fulfillment of your desire. This is by no means easy, as all our life we have depended on things and conditions around us for the fulfillment of our desires.

The solution to this difficulty is to train the mind to obey you. To remind the mind all the time that your *Consciousness is the Creator*, everything is made of Consciousness and the substance of everything is Consciousness, your Consciousness is the same as Universal Consciousness and finally, that you are Consciousness and not the mind. The mind is only the distributor of the stuff of Consciousness with which everything is made. The easiest way to achieve this state of mind is to keep on meditating on the Four Proclamations.

Imagination emerges from your Consciousness and then it is processed through your mind. Your mind is prone to relating to external conditions to assess whether your present circumstances can accomplish your Intention. If the mind cannot find a reference point in the past, it will reject the Imagination and consider it as a fantasy. The mind has a tendency to lean on familiarity.

When you have trained your mind to realize that whatever you have imagined is your reality regardless of the external conditions, then only will it accept, then only can you dwell in your Imagination and bring in the mighty force of concentration and form your Vision. This attitude of mind is very succinctly portrayed by George Bernard Shaw, the great thinker and playwright, in his play *Back to Methuselah* in which the Serpent says to Eve,

When you and Adam talk, I hear you say 'Why?' Always 'Why?' You see things; and you say 'Why?' But I dream things that never were; and I say 'Why not?'

When you have Mastered your mind by meditation you will know that your Imagination is the mirror of your Consciousness and the world around you is the reflection of your Imagination. What you see, you imagine, and what you imagine, you create.

Step Three: Vision

Imagination is like a river that flows towards its goal of Manifestation. Your Intention is the source of the stream of your Imagination. The goal of the flow of the stream of Imagination is to fulfill your Desire. Your Desire becomes your Consciousness. You form the picture of your Desire.

Imagination in the beginning gushes out of your Intention in a mad chaos. It is totally disorganized. Then with the mind's eye you organize and order the chaos of the Imagination into form; you see it in all its details, color, sound, taste, smell, and touch; you have formed the Vision that you can focus on. This is the force and the working power behind all physical Manifestation.

St. Paul gives a vivid idea of how vision is realized and manifested in his Epistle to the Hebrews,

Now faith is the substance of things hoped for, the evidence of things not seen.

- Hebrews 11:1

He also states that God framed the worlds the same way. In the following verse he says,

> *Through faith we understand that the worlds were framed by the word of God, so that things which are seen were not made of things which do appear.*
>
> - Hebrews 11:3

The word Faith sometimes conjures up disbelief and uncertainty. St. Paul diffuses this idea and shows that your Vision, what you hoped for, is actual substance, and is not made of things which appear and your senses have not experienced. It is a Vision.

To confirm and weed out the belief that Faith is relying on some arbitrary deity on whose moods or whims we need to depend on for what we ask, St. Paul emphasizes that God also framed the worlds the same way with *The Word.* Word is thought and thought is Vision. Faith is to know that what you hoped for is your Vision; it is real and it is already yours. It's a certainty and you don't require any evidence or proof.

You will also notice St. Paul did not say that God created the worlds; he said that God *framed* the worlds. A frame is a picture, a Vision. If we look deeper into his statements you will notice he confirms Hermes's dictum, "As the Macrocosm so the Microcosm and as the Microcosm so the Macrocosm," and the Vedic aphorism, "As the Universe so the Individual and as the Individual so the Universe." The Universe creates worlds as the individual creates his worlds.

Faith is total reliance on Consciousness, on an elevated reason beyond the capacity of the mind, which is subject to the five senses.

Science has been stumped by matter. Science has to this day not been able to explain whether matter is a No-Thing or if it is a thing, and if so, where does it come from? Similarly, mind does not understand the power behind Manifestation.

Your Consciousness is not time and space bound. It is free from the past, present, and the future, which is the realm of the mind. The stuff of Vision is Consciousness. You cannot Vision in the past and you know you cannot Vision in the present; it is too fleeting a moment to do so, and you cannot Vision in the future; you can only Vision in the Absolute and your Vision is not subject to any contingency or condition. Therefore it is already yours. You go about your daily life knowing that you already have it. It is no longer a make-believe world, it is real. Your Vision is your reality.

We know that Universal Consciousness is the forming power throughout the Universe and we don't need any proof of that, we just have to look around us. When we look up in the sky at night and see the beauty and the glory of the stars and then we see the beauty of the rose and its perfection, enchantment becomes our Being.

Individual Consciousness is identical to Universal Consciousness. It is the same. The Individual is the drop of the ocean and the Universe is the ocean and in the drop, is the ocean. The Universe is the blaze and the Individual is the spark. The spark has the same power as the blaze and they are identical; the spark can create the same blaze.

Everything in the world works on the principle of Cause and Effect, it is an unfailing law. Your Vision is the Cause and the tangible Manifestation of the Vision is an inevitable effect. Your expectancy of receiving the tangible Manifestation is indispensable to having your Vision manifest.

Guard your thoughts and meditate on the Four Proclamations. Know you already have it. It will take assiduous practice. Persist and it will become your habit; success is a habit.

Step Four: Manifestation

The completion of Vision is physical Manifestation. In the allegories of creation and in the Ancient texts, Manifestation is given the term *Earth*. These allegories are stories that tell us how we form Visions and manifest our Visions. The *Bible* begins, "In the beginning God created the heaven and the earth. And the earth was without form and void;"(Genesis 1:1-2) And we notice a stark anomaly here; How can earth be void and without form? A thing has a form. The message is deeply hidden in this one statement. A thing cannot be void. It is ridiculous to think that a thing can be void. Then we must examine, why does the Author clearly say that the earth was void and without form?

All the riches of the Universe are hidden in this *Void* and in this *Earth* that is *without form*. We must dig and find the message. The message is encrypted by having it exposed. It is laid before our eyes so obviously that it challenges our intelligence to decipher it. The obvious is what the genius sees and which the ordinary ignores.

The earth is in the Vision. The Vision is the real and the earth is the embodiment of the Vision. It is void in the Vision and it is without form in the Vision. The Author of the *Bible* clearly tells us the real is the Vision and the earth is only the Manifestation. The Manifestation is already in the Vision. The tree is in the seed. If you cut open the seed you won't see the tree. You know the tree is void and without form and it is still in the seed, with all its leaves and branches.

When you Vision, you already have what you want and it is without form and void. It is your earth. Every form in this Universe is only an embodiment of Consciousness. You are Consciousness and your Consciousness creates your reality.

This is how God created and this is how we create. We know that heaven is within us and heaven within us is our Consciousness.

The real is the Vision and a Vision of what you want is without form and void; it is. Manifestation is inevitable.

In the *Vedas*, *Brahman* created the world by Visioning. The stories of Creation are metaphors of how you create and bring your Vision into Manifestation.

The circumference of the Circle is the Manifestation of the center of the Circle. The circumference is the center of the circle expanded and yet we know that the center has no dimension. It has no magnitude or length, breadth and height. It is In-Visible and it is without form and void. We also know that there cannot be a circle without a center. The Circumference is the center, which is without form and void.

All tangible things are made out of matter and we know that matter when reduced to its ultimate, becomes No-Thing. Science calls it energy, which is vibration. The question is what is vibrating? We need a particle to vibrate with and when matter is reduced to No-Thing there are no particles.

Your concentration on your Vision forms the material Manifestation. Concentration is the force of the center. A concentrated mind soars into the world of the real; concentration takes it to the realm of the unknown. It opens up worlds that we were not aware of, yet we have been living in them. Now we know it and have control over it and we create the world of our Conscious choosing.

Then we know the word *impossible* describes our state of mind and we can change our state of mind. Then we will know that *I and the Universe are One* and *All things are possible with God.*

Manifestation is in the Vision.

The Poem Two Birds

The following poem from my childhood has lingered in my heart to this day. This poem by the great Nobel Laureate Poet Rabindranath Tagore is one I have heard over and over again and it has served as a guide post in my life. The spirit of this poem has led me to make many decisions which I am happy about, though the situations were hard.

I don't know if it is possible to do justice to this poem by translating it from its original language, my mother tongue, Bengali. I, with all humility, ask the Great Poet, Rabrindranth Tagore to forgive me if I have not done justice to his masterpiece. I hope the reader will find the same strength and the same joy that I have found from this poem.

CHAPTER 21

THE STORY OF TWO BIRDS

A Love Story of the Soul and the Mind

This is the story of two birds, one that was living in a golden cage and the other who was living free in the forest. Somehow by the wondrous work of the Almighty they met and fell in love.

It is a mystery what the Almighty had in Its mind.

The bird of the forest told the bird of the cage, “Come, let’s fly away free to the forest together.”

The bird of the cage said to the bird of the forest, “Come stay with me in the cage, it is comforting, secure and well protected.”

The bird of the forest said, “No, I will not let myself be caged and shackled.”

The bird of the cage replied, "How can I go to the forest? I can't."

So the bird of the forest sat outside the cage and sang the songs of freedom of the forest. The bird of the cage sat in its golden cage and sang the songs it had been taught to sing.

"Why don't you sing the songs of the forest, the songs of freedom?" asked the bird of the forest.

"Why don't you learn the songs of the cage?" replied the bird of the cage.

The bird of the forest said, "No, I don't want to sing taught songs. I don't want to sing songs you were made to sing. I want to sing the songs of my heart."

"How can I sing songs of the forest?" asked the bird of the cage.

The bird of the forest said, "Look up at the open sky, absolutely clear blue. There are no limits anywhere."

The bird of the cage responded, "Look at this golden cage; it is furnished, neat and tidy and secure."

The bird of the forest sighed, "Let go of yourself. Release yourself amidst the clouds and spread your wings and fly with me and feel the freedom."

The bird of the cage heaved, "I am in this place of comfort, luxury and well protected where there is no trouble. Come, live with me and enjoy the security and all the comforts that go with it."

"No, I cannot live in your golden cage. There is nowhere to fly," said the bird of the forest.

The bird of the cage replied, "How can I go with you to the clouds? There is nowhere to sit on the clouds."

This is a tale of two birds that fell in love with each other but could not reconcile their feelings. They were in love but they could not be together. Between the rods of the cage they touched each other's face. They looked at each other's eyes. But one could not understand the other or convince the other of the freedom of the forest or the luxury of the cage.

They stayed alone in their own worlds and hit their wings against the cage to feel each other and to love. And with great pain, the bird of the cage, hitting its wings against the cage asked, "Come closer."

The bird of the forest, full of agony replied, "No, if I come closer the cage door might close and I won't ever be free again."

The bird of the cage with a heavy submissive sigh said, "I don't have the strength to fly."

Translation in prose form of Rabindranath Tagore's Bengali poem *Two Birds*.

CHAPTER 22

AWAKENING FROM THE SELF IMPOSED DREAM

Epilogue

We have come into this world to experience what we have never experienced before. We have come to reach out and feel all that we can feel, all that we have never felt before. Once we have accomplished that, we will have paid homage to our life.

As long as we are not bold enough to step out into the unknown and experience life to its fullest, we will feel bored. We will be caught up in the confusion of existence. Then existence will become a burden for us.

We have an innate, intense urge to touch the ends of this Universe and know who we are in this dream of existence. We are asleep in a dream state and we are entrapped in a dream, struggling to awaken yet afraid to awaken, afraid to leave our dream, because we feel it to be our reality.

We must release ourselves from this self imposed dream that surrounds us at this moment, and form a Vision of the reality that we truly desire. We must apply the Ancient Secrets of Success to create a life full of abundance and joy. A life we are meant to live that befits our Divinity and our Unity, which is our Oneness. We are the Universe.

The Longing of the Unlit Lamp

The lamp stood unlit in the dark.
Darkness was its world.
Darkness was its Universe.

The lamp knew not,
What its purpose was.
Darkness covered all its yearnings
To find its purpose.

Then, when anguish reached
Its limit of pain,
It cried out to its Creator:

"Pain of purposelessness overwhelms me.
Come to me, my Master, my Creator,
Show me the reason."

Then the lamp itself lit the lamp.
Darkness vanished.
Purpose, mission realized -
Love...

Join Our Mailing List So We Can Continue Supporting You Through Newsletters, Webinars and Upcoming Events

We advise you to register your name, email address, city and country at https://tulshisen.com/client and we will keep in touch with you with all the upcoming information and events of Tulshi Sen Consulting including letting you know if we are coming to your part of the world.

Congratulations, in obtaining the *Ancient Secrets of Success.* Here at Tulshi Sen Consulting we have been helping people around the world in their careers, businesses and professions. We are available to help you if you need it in developing your own success plan in your own chosen vocation.

To enhance and expedite the effect of this book watch the following video on YouTube which shows you how we are held back in life involuntarily:

Breaking the Chain that holds Our Mind -
https://youtu.be/UqlkHzKoPPU - 4 min. 25 sec.

We welcome you to contact us for any other requirements by going to our website at https://tulshisen.com or contacting us at service@tulshisen.com .